"WHEN THE MARINER has been tossed for many days in thick weather, and on an unknown sea, he naturally avails himself of the first pause in the storm, the earliest glance of the sun, to take his latitude, and ascertain how far the elements have driven him from his true course. Let us imitate this prudence, and, before we float farther on the waves of this debate, refer to the point from which we departed, that we may at least be able to conjecture where we now are."

—Daniel Webster, *Second Reply to Senator Hayne*
January 26–27, 1830

100 DAYS

IN THE LIFE OF

Rutherford Hayes

ERIC EBINGER

ORANGE *frazer* PRESS
Wilmington, Ohio

Published for the author by:
Orange Frazer Press
P.O. Box 214
Wilmington, OH 45177

Telephone: 937.382.3196 for price and shipping information.
Website: www.orangefrazer.com

Book and cover design: Alyson Rua and Orange Frazer Press

Front cover photograph, from left to right: Webb Cook Hayes, Lucy
Hayes, R.W. Huntington, Fanny Hayes, President Hayes, Rutherford Platt Hayes. In front of photo, Adda (Cook) Huntington.

Front flap photograph: The Hayes Home, "Spiegel Grove,"
Fremont, Ohio. Photo by Eric Ebinger.

Library of Congress Control Number: 2016938832

For Mom and Dad,
Gary and Judy

for every "No,"
and every "Yes,"
and even the occasional,
"Because I said so."

Acknowledgments

Writing is a strange process. Thoughts come at all times of day and during all circumstances—recorded on napkins, receipts, and Post It Notes and scattered on nightstands, desktops, and passenger seats. Words begat sentences which begat paragraphs as the process becomes unbearably lonesome, save the people those words, sentences, and paragraphs are attempting to bring to life.

Through the loneliness comes special individuals who lighten the load. To the following I owe a considerable debt of gratitude:

The staff at the remarkable Library and Museum of Rutherford B. Hayes at Spiegel Grove in Fremont, Ohio.

The staff at the Ohio History Center in Columbus, Ohio.

The staff of the United States Library of Congress.

To Marcy Hawley and Sarah Hawley, the words of Jim Henson come to mind, "There's not a word yet, for old friends, who've just met." Your kindness, grace and understanding have been calming and assuring. I am so thankful my "passion" is in your hands.

Thank you to Chris Price, Karen Krupp, Anne Lowery, Yvonne Taylor, Ruth Earl, Jan Gessner, Denise Wyatt, my amazing parents Gary and Judy, my sisters Wendy and Dawn, my Grandpa Dale Ebinger, Aunt Jennie and Aunt Julia.

And to my Grandparents who continue to inspire me from beyond: Grandma Great and Grandad, Grandpa Bud, Grandma Betty, and Grandma Jean.

And to my wife Misty, the bearer of the significant burden of this writer's loneliness—I cannot, at the end of such a project, begin to find the words to express my gratitude. You are my Lucy.

Contents

Note on Sources

The *Diary and Letters of Rutherford B. Hayes* are the backbone of this work. The richness in detail and depth are striking. Each paragraph, from beginning to end, serve the reader a unique blend of drama, wit, and completeness of thought on every subject and experience of Hayes' life such that this author finds it unnerving, and unnecessary, to condense. The excerpts from Rutherford Hayes come from his diary and letters available to the world online at the Hayes Library and Museum website at www.rbhayes.org.

Each 'day' in Hayes' life is accompanied by a letter or diary entry. Both primary sources have not been edited for spelling or grammar, though they are largely unblemished.

Grateful thanks to the Rutherford B. Hayes Library and Museum for making such literary treasures available to the general public online. May this work but open a window to more research and further study of one of the most important, and unfortunately discarded, figures of the nineteenth century.

Preface

This book is not intended to replace previous extensive and glorious biographies of Rutherford B. Hayes. All research on Hayes should begin with the thoughtful biographers Ari Hoogenboom and Harry Barnard, but with respectful nods toward William Charles Smith for the earliest impeccably researched work on Hayes. This author does not intend to replace those works as they stand alone in their worth on the Hayes life, legacy, and scholarship.

100 Days in the Life of Rutherford Hayes is intended to focus additional light on our 19th President and compel, even for a short period, the Lincoln, Washington, Kennedy, and Roosevelt enthusiasts to a better understanding of Hayes and to allow that light to expand in the misunderstood and forgotten era between the icons of Old Abe and the Bull Moose.

Between them, Rutherford B. Hayes is lost. Where Washington, Lincoln, and the Roosevelts rule the historical rankings, and Buchanan and Tyler, and Hayes's Ohio neighbor Harding elicit tomes on failure, Hayes is adrift among past presidents of the United States, harboring neither ill will nor promotion.

There are no Hayes Memorials in Washington. There are no films showcasing his life's moments to the masses. His birthplace is not a monument but a brick in front of a gas station.

In 1948, Arthur Schlesinger Jr. paralleled America's interest in ranking college football teams with the presidents, and created a ladder of greatness by which all historians began to judge the nation's top executive. With all due respect to the man who brought us important and intimate portraits of Franklin Roosevelt, Andrew Jackson, and Robert Kennedy, he ruined presidential scholarship by forcing us to place one president ahead of another, and mercifully rank some of them extremely low.

What the ranking does not allow is how a Truman might have handled the Great Depression, how a Kennedy might have guided us through a Civil War, or how a Polk, yes, a Polk, might have reacted to the attack on September 11, 2001.

By forcing the ranking, we lose the opportunity to weigh each president based on their unique vantage point. Lincoln should not be compared to Washington, or for that matter ranked higher or lower based on his respective actions in completely different historical spheres.

And in just the same sentence, Rutherford Hayes should not be compared to Lincoln. As early as November 1861, Rutherford Hayes was pressing for Emancipation. As a Major in the 23rd Regiment of Ohio Volunteers, Hayes was far ahead of Lincoln in calling for the absolute freeing of all slaves. However, Hayes reported such from his vantage point at his winter quarters in Fayetteville, Maryland. Lincoln, of course, had an entirely different point of view from his desk in the Executive Mansion.

On some levels, it is a scholarly exercise to rank presidents. We can probably all agree Washington, Lincoln and Franklin Roosevelt belong at the top. But in 1962, Schlesinger ranked Eisenhower, who had just left office, near the bottom at #22. Today, more than fifty years since the close of his administration, he ranks the highest at #7. What changed? It certainly was not Eisenhower.

It is here on these rankings once again, Rutherford Birchard Hayes is lost, stuck in the middle whether in 1948 or 2016. Even in popular opinion polls, Hayes is on a middle rung of the ladder.

Much has been written concerning how a character is shaped. George Washington experienced vast and substantial failures in his early career in the military, and also in the Revolution. Abraham Lincoln failed miserably in politics again and again, which came on the heels of repeated failures in business. And Franklin Roosevelt, should polio be considered a physical failure, endured an emotional battle the likes of which is unimaginable.

Each of these men experienced different categories of failure, and each of them later in life steered the country through difficult times of its own. The fires forged in the depths of defeat made them steadfast and unmoved in the face of great adversity. Although it probably didn't comfort them at the time, such a fire (failure) would bear fruit of utmost importance to the masses looking to them for leadership.

Included here are 100 days which defined Rutherford B. Hayes. Such a list, similar to the sentiments joined by the ranking of presidents, will no doubt elicit much discussion. All will be served because it will cause discussions of the very important life of Rutherford Hayes.

Finally, the book is laid out in days that 'defined' Rutherford B. Hayes. Simply put, these are the days that stand out. These are the days which, in his early life, his resolve was either fueled or tested. And in later years, these are the days where the true character of the man was revealed.

Rutherford Hayes will not disappoint you.

Days that define a man or woman are not easy. They are not vacations, days spent reading, or days in the midst of the mire and muck of a work day. Days that shape the character of a man who will be president are hard, awful, miserable days where crises rise up and need to be met. Hayes himself, starting very young, was fond of saying that boldness must meet your enterprises. If you act boldly, meet hardship boldly, you will ensure your success.

It takes a confident, perhaps even arrogant man to consider himself worthy and capable of being president. Such confidence is not born of men seeking to be president. It is cured in the fires of the kiln.

Rutherford Hayes was elected president under extraordinary circumstances. Having failed to receive a majority of the popular vote, Hayes encountered a long battle, right up to three days before his Inauguration, forever in doubt whether he would in fact become president, or Samuel Tilden, the other candidate whose name, though popular at the time, has been lost to history.

Hayes was, in the estimate of most historians and authors, an average president. But this book presents him just like Washington, Lincoln, and FDR, the perfect man for the tumultuous time he was president.

Presidents, by their very nature, do not shrink from responsibility or crisis, and Hayes was no different. It is quite astounding, when measuring the man on his exploits in the Civil War alone, that he is not heralded among military geniuses alongside Eisenhower, Patton, and Pershing.

One can argue every day of your life is an expectation for one future, major crisis. And through the first thirty years of Hayes life, there was no indication he would be, or ever wanted to be, President of the United States. But that fact has made this effort all the more interesting.

This is the story of Hayes in the fire.

100 DAYS

IN THE LIFE OF

Rutherford Hayes

Early life...

"How true is the old proverb that 'delay is the thief of time.'
Almost a week has passed since I commenced this diary and the
first page still remains to be written. Neither want of time nor
inclination has occasioned this neglect, but simply the habit of
putting off till tomorrow what should be done today. I have, it is
true, had nothing of importance to relate, but if I make it a rule
not to write till something of moment occurs, I fear my diary
would end where it commenced."

— *Rutherford B. Hayes, age 19, diary, June 17, 1841*

JULY 20, 1822, DELAWARE, OHIO

Death was common on the Ohio prairie in 1822. Cholera, yellow fever, malaria, and smallpox decimated families both small and large, leaving children, orphans, and parents childless. Sickness knew not race or economic boundaries. It was mercifully unjust in its choosing.

The worst offender of the prairie family was typhoid fever. Forty years before the dreaded disease killed more soldiers than bullets in the Civil War, it passed through the small town of Delaware, thirty miles north of the new, but now third, capital city of the Buckeye State, Columbus.

Three hundred and sixty-nine people lived in Delaware according to the 1820 census. Rutherford and Sophia Hayes were looking forward to welcoming another member to their growing family. Like many parents on the prairie, Rutherford and Sophia had already lost one child at birth and were still reeling from the death of their four-year-old daughter in 1821. Raising a family on the prairie was slow and unforgiving. They looked forward to the birth of their next child with hope, and a little bit of fear.

On July 20, 1822, typhoid fever curled its way through the house and struck the patriarch. He died at age thirty-five, leaving his wife six months pregnant and son Lorenzo and daughter Fanny, fatherless.

Sophia would come to rely heavily on her younger brother Sardis, who was described as "wild" by Hayes biographer Ari Hoogenboom, during the trek from their settlement in New England to Ohio in 1816.

Without a father from the start, Rutherford "Rud" Hayes could have led a life quite different than lawyer, soldier, politician, and president. Indeed his childhood could have been quite different if not for the close bond between his mother and her own brother, who began to look after his niece and nephews as if they were his own children. Uncle Sardis would supply the family with money throughout the rest of his life.

Although it is possible to reflect that had his father lived, Rutherford's life would have pursued a much different path, so we begin the selection of 'days' in this book with an event that caused more impact on the rest than any other, the day young Rutherford's father died on July 20, 1822.

OCTOBER 4, 1822, DELAWARE, OHIO, BIRTHDAY

Imagine the heartbreak and joy Sophia Hayes experienced, welcoming her second son into the world. It was a terrifying, empty world without her husband of nine years. Her son would share his name, and the same auburn hair and blue eyes.

"Rud" (as he would become known as a boy) was not out of the woods when he was born. Deaths of infants were common in 1822, and Rutherford Sr. and Sophia had lost their first son in 1814. Hayes was born "feeble," probably due to his Mother's stress caused by the loss of her husband and the duties of handling the household alone. According to biographer Ari Hoogenboom, Sophia anguished over her son for the first two years of his life.[1]

Birthplace of Rutherford Birchard Hayes, Delaware, Ohio, 1822.

Rud and his sister, Fanny, were the only surviving children of Rutherford and Sophia, as each of the other siblings were lost to disease or accident before they turned ten. Perhaps the two-year mark of anguish was a common turbulent time for young children on the Ohio prairie. In the coming decades, Rutherford and future wife, Lucy, would lose three of their eight children before their second birthday.

1. Hoogenboom, Ari, *Rutherford B. Hayes, Warrior & President*, (Lawrence, Kansas, University Press of Kansas, 1995), 8.

JANUARY 20, 1825, DELAWARE, OHIO, THE MILLPOND

"He was kind and good natured—prompt, energetic and courageous and the earliest protector of his little sister."
—*Hayes on his brother, Lorenzo, July, 1856*

Like most young boys on the prairie, Lorenzo Hayes enjoyed the rambunctiousness that accompanies limitless possibilities in adventure and exploring. Delaware was ripe with woods, fields, streams and of course the Olentangy River with its numberless opportunities to romp and stomp on the banks.

You can imagine Lorenzo and his friends hiking and fishing and skipping rocks across the millpond. And you can imagine them ice skating in the winter. Lorenzo broke through the ice on the millpond on January 20, 1825, and drowned.

As common as death was on the prairie, there is no question the loss of Lorenzo caused considerable pain in the household. Rutherford Hayes was less than thirty months old, but in an instant he became the man of the house.

October 31, 1838, Gambier, Ohio, The Road to College

"You said in your letter to Uncle Austin that Mr. Webb had written to you about my staying here another year. If [I] thought it would be a great advantage to me I had rather stay, but I don't think it would; for persons who have been through college say that when a person enters college so that he can get on the first year very easy, after that [he] don't get along so well as those who have to work hard when they first enter.

If I don't enter college till a year, I'll have to stay a year longer in college and that year spent in studying human nature would be more profitably [spent] than studying dead languages. Things being so, I had rather not stay another year...

If you think it best that I should stay a year longer, I am perfectly willing to do it without going home."

—Hayes to Uncle Sardis as he neared the end of his secondary schooling in Middletown, Connecticut, 1838.

College was available to very few in 1838. Kenyon College, located in Gambier, Ohio, in Knox County, was the first private college in the Buckeye State. Although his Uncle Sardis had planned on Hayes going to Harvard, his mother, Sophia, had encouraged Hayes to enter the much closer Kenyon.

The significance of this day in Hayes's life is not that it is the first time he has been away from home. Hayes had spent the last few years away from home at school, first at Norwalk, Ohio, at a Methodist Academy and then at Middletown, Connecticut.

He contemplated not continuing his education after the boredom he suffered in Norwalk. In Middletown, the tutelage of Isaac Webb (no relation to future wife Lucy Webb) at Webb's exclusive private school instilled an appreciation for learning that was missing in earlier attempts.

If Hayes thought the forty-mile journey from Delaware to Gambier was particularly challenging, he did not mention it in his diary. Only two sentences remain from the trip, one stating he spent time in Mount Vernon on his way to college on October 31 and on November 1, 1838, Hayes notes just one sentence more, "Arrived at Gambier; looks as I expected."

Perhaps he recorded the only thoughts of a sixteen-year-old boy who had already seen his share of the United States at the time. But it was a significant journey, forty miles on foot that took him two days, leaving one life for another—ending the education of his youth for the education of a man. Unfortunately, the richness of his diary and letters do not reveal his thoughts on his arduous flight. But we can argue it was an exciting moment when he stepped foot on the property.

November 27, 1838, Kenyon College, Gambier, Ohio, Skating Pond

"Went skating for the first time and broke through the thin ice where the water was eight feet deep; was not scared much. My companions helped me out without much trouble. I could have got up without any help."

—*Hayes, diary*

Hayes was at school less than a month when he and his friends ventured to the local skating pond. We do not know how long he skated, but he found a weak spot in the ice and fell through. Hayes himself was dismissive in his journal and letters of the near-catastrophe, perhaps part bravado and part serious.

The experience must have shocked the freshman. His friends helped pull him out, though he admitted later he could have raised himself out if he had been alone. History books, with all due respect, tend to give such activities only a sentence or two as the recording of the fact and not much else. It is seldom the purpose of the historian to proselytize on the impact of the event, merely to report the facts. But there would have been significant fervor surrounding this event. Hayes would first have been helped out of the pond. He and his friends would have then rushed to his dormitory at the top of "Old Kenyon."

His clothes would need changed, and he would need dried off. Finally, clothes would need to be put back on and the long slow process of bringing him out of his freezing state. In 1838, fire was the only way to warm the body besides layers of clothing and exercise itself.

More questions remain. Did he tell his companions his brother drowned in such an event? Did his friends check on him periodically during the evening?

His letters home do not reveal the event was any more than an unfortunate circumstance, suggesting, perhaps to keep his mother from worrying or remembering, that it was nothing. Hoogenboom explains the entire episode is, for Hayes, an "exercise in self-discipline."[1]

After returning home during the Christmas holiday, Hayes reported in his diary that he "went skating as usual." Is it possible, immediately following his accident, he returned to the spot his brother perished?

The skates which belonged to Lorenzo are on display at the Hayes Presidential Center in Fremont, Ohio, a stunning reminder of the eternal youth of young Lorenzo, and perhaps also the resolve of "Rud" to keep skating.

---

1. Hoogenboom, Ari, *Rutherford B. Hayes, Warrior & President*, (Lawrence, Kansas, University Press of Kansas, 1995), 27.

There were but three individuals in the Hayes household after Lorenzo broke through the ice in 1825. Letters to and from Hayes and his mother and sister suggest, in sometimes hilarious wit, the closeness of their bonds. Lucky are we that Hayes spent some of the formative days of his youth away at school and that letters survive to tell the tales. The exchanges are priceless:

"I see you are so much obliged to me for five words that you cannot express it, and now, of course, you'll be so much obliged to me that you'll sneeze, gap [gape], and other omens of the kind. Don't congratulate yourself too much about my making short sermons when I am a preacher. If you had seen some documents that proceeded from my pen, you'd be congratulating yourself on the idea of what a long time you'd have to sleep in sermons. I must say something about gaping. You need not try to save any for me, for if you do your mouth will be open all the time…"

—Rud to Fanny, February 5, 1839

The letters from Hayes to his homestead refer continually to "Uncle said" and "Fanny said," etc. Imagine the household mentioning to each other they were writing Rud and each one of them at different times saying, "Oh, tell him this, tell him that."

"You said Uncle said 'I must not walk home in a day.' Well, it is immaterial. I'd as soon be a minute or two over a day as under. But what pleased me particularly was your saying I must 'bring my clothes home,' as if I would forget to wear any. You say I missed seeing many friends by not being home, but if I had not been here I should not have seen some of my friends, for instance Mr. Sparrow or Mr. Dyer, etc. [His professors]

Uncle will get a letter at the end of the session from old Sparrow and I reckon it will say I am a tolerable good boy, considering my birthplace."

—*Rud to Mother Sophia, March 10, 1839*

Sarcasm from a teenage boy off at college in 1839. Mothers and fathers of today, take note and relax.

Finally, this wonderful paragraph from Hayes to his sister on the choice of her writing instrument:

"I am astonished at your cruelty in preferring quills to steel pens, for in using a steel pen you are assisting thousands of poor souls to gain their bread, viz., ironmongers, miners, blacksmiths, etc., who gain their living by making steel pens; but on the other hand you would reflect upon the pain of Madame Goose and Mr. Gander in having their feathers plucked out by the roots. Oh! it is horrid to think on, tho I am now using quills myself.

I hope to be home if nothing happens on Saturday the 23d of March. I don't know whether I shall write any more or not.

I remain your affectionate brother, R. B. Hayes"

—*Rud to Fanny, undated*

One hundred fifty years from now, we will have no treasure trove of personal literature by which to research future presidents. It will all be lost in a cascade of Facebook posts and texts.

As the letters suggest, Rud adored his sister, Fanny. In 1839, with Rud still spending most of his time at Kenyon, Fanny met a man in Columbus by the name of William Augustus Platt. They became engaged to be married in the summer of 1839 and planned a winter wedding. Sophia broke the news to Rud in a letter dated July 20, 1839. After referencing the anniversary of his father's death, she told Rud his sister was marrying.

Rud did not reply. A letter came from Fanny a few days later, full of the wit, sarcasm, and sprite that characterized all their correspondence. Suspecting a conversation took place between Sophia and Fanny, both of the women asked Rud to 'try' to like William.

The shock of his sister's marriage alone was understandable. But there was also something else in the letter. The fact that Hayes would have to move into Platt's house was the additional burden he was not quite willing to accept. Even though his Uncle Sardis Birchard was his legal guardian, Rutherford was the only male in the house for long periods of time.

Perhaps we can assume, though Hayes was gracious and polite throughout his life, that the seventeen-year-old enjoyed a certain notoriety, if not, respect for being the head of the Hayes house. Obviously, his sentiment to his diary, "I am no longer Lord of the Manor," speaks volumes to his perceived drop in value.

It should also be noted, Hayes had not yet met Platt. On top of the news of the marriage itself and his demotion in the house, he also probably felt offended that a decision was made for marriage without consultation of the brother.

Everything considered, this was a shock that caused Hayes much angst. When a seventeen-year-old male encounters news he does not like, he has two choices. 1. He can 'spout off' or 2. He can digest it and accept it. By waiting two weeks to respond to both his mother and Fanny, Hayes appears to have digested the news. Perhaps, we can imply, the young man waited because he was indeed angry and perhaps hurt. But knowing the strength of his character, we can appreciate the fact that the two weeks of silence most likely saved a great deal of hurt feelings on Fanny's side, and perhaps setting out on the wrong foot with his new brother-in-law, too.

Later during his presidency, he advised those closest to him never to respond immediately to upsetting news. The lesson was learned very early.

December 2, 1840, Kenyon College, The Election of William Henry Harrison

On June 25, 1840, Hayes began a comprehensive and detailed history of the presidential contest of the same year. The election, with General William Henry Harrison facing President Martin Van Buren, was a gripping national contest that, according to Hayes researcher, Charles Richard Williams, "Never before had the people been so generally stirred."

Hayes followed the contest closely. He recorded the contests state by state, making predictions based on previous elections. When the final results were in, Hayes announced:

"November 5—The long agony is over. The 'whirlwind' has swept over the land and General Harrison is undoubtedly elected President. I never was more elated by anything in my life. His majority in this State about sixteen acres, or twenty-three thousand. Kentucky and everywhere else is going fine. Glorious!"

Hayes took great delight that President Van Buren was relegated to a vote total equal to that of a lesser third party candidate, but the significance of the experience came earlier in the final entry, "I never was more elated by anything in my life." Of course, Hayes was only eighteen years old at this writing, but the statement is fact. And perhaps his admiration for Harrison as well as a boyhood worship of George Washington would stoke in him the fires of military bravery and political fervor.

Though the future was cloudy for Hayes, on this day the winner he backed passionately had won and the taste of political success danced in his mouth.

Harrison passed away one month following the longest Inaugural Address in history. John Tyler assumed the presidency and soon caused great strife among the Whigs by vetoing the bank bill, designed to create a stable currency.

Hayes recorded:

"I was never more rejoiced than when it was ascertained that Harrison's election was certain. I hoped we should then have a stable currency of uniform value; but since Tyler has vetoed one way of accomplishing this, I would not hesitate to try others. So much for politics, in which I have ceased to take an interest. My hopes and wishes were all realized in the election of old General Harrison, and I am [glad] to be able to say that I am now indifferent to such things."

—*Hayes, diary, September 6, 1841*

Quite a sudden change of heart. But he is, after all, still a teenager.

COLUMBUS, OHIO, APRIL 17, 1841, FANNY FALLEN ILL

"Gambier, Ohio, July 19, 1840,

Dear Sister: I can but look back with 'fear and trembling' upon my folly in writing a letter characterized by such a foolhardy disregard of consequences as was my last; for among the first lessons taught me in my childhood was to shun everything like an attempt to startle or frighten a fellow-being for the sake of a moment's fun or a senseless laugh. Yet forgetting or disregarding this oft-repeated warning, I, as if goaded on by a demon, concocted, reduced to writing, and mailed to you a letter of three pages' length. 'My tongue cleaves to the roof of my mouth,' my knees knock together, and my hands refuse to perform their office when a glimmering of the jeopardy in which your reason and life was placed by that letter crosses my brain.

Thanks to the soundness of your education, the strength of your intellect, and the firmness of your soul, you are saved; and believe me when I say that never, never, never again shall I run such immanent hazard of blighting forever all the happiness which our family now enjoys by writing a letter of such unusual length.

You and your little band of emigrants have by this time settled a colony in the northern part of that heathenish city, 'about equally distant from the penitentiary, graveyard, rope-walk, and slaughter-house…'"

—*Rud to Fanny*

After a paragraph complementing Fanny on her new family and advising how to make them viable, he ended the letter with a series of random thoughts:

"Miscellany:

Commencement is on Wednesday, the 5th of August.

We had a fine time on the Fourth. Eight students got into a snap and were put on probation, two of them professors of religion. One had to read a confession to escape dismission. [sic]

Mrs. Hayes is expected here the first of next month. Mr. and Mrs. Platt also.

Money is scarce and much needed, as the bankrupt law is defeated in the H. R. [House of Representatives].

By the end of the session R. B. H. must have thirty-five dollars. One installment of which is expected and needed in his next letter from home.

The mail will be closed in ten minutes.

A letter is requested immediately.

Ten more words is wanted to fill out this column.

Mother wishes me to keep my hair, 'teeth,' and nails cut short.

Your brother, R. Birchard Hayes
Give my respects to the family."

Hayes overcame his shock and perhaps anger at the engagement and impending wedding of his sister. The teasing and affection continued in his letters and he looked forward amorously to the large family William and Fanny would create together.

Unfortunately, his joy at Fanny's new beginning would be short lived. He would discover his sister was sick in April, 1842. She was later admitted to an insane asylum. The letters to his brother-in-law were heartbreaking:

"Gambier, April 25, 1842,

My Dear Brother: Ever since you first informed me of the critical situation of our dear Fanny I have entertained the most anxious fears for her safety. Yours of the 22d, which I have just received, has not diminished them. She has such a feeble constitution she cannot endure but little. I hope the treatment she will receive…will be of benefit. Do let me hear from you or Mother as often as possible, if you write but three lines. Under the most favorable circumstances, I presume from what you said that we shall be in suspense for a great while…I have no fears but she will have all done for her that is in the power of human aid…I am in good health as usual. There is nothing of interest here. All our friends are well. Bryan has just been in. Presents his love to all. In haste.

Your affectionate brother, R. B. H."

In a letter following on May 31, Hayes tries to explain to his brother-in-law that he feels an emptiness when thinking of Fanny that perhaps is similar to the emptiness of the house with her absent. He is probably trying to help, and trying to convince Platt he is distraught. Hayes ends the letter writing, "But I speak too much of this. You suffer enough I know already. I should not mention it."

Fanny would recover, but the experience left an indelible mark on Hayes. His work and affection for the sick and invalids of society during his political career were constant heralds to his sister. One closing letter to his brother-in-law records grief most of the time left unwritten, "Do excuse brevity. I have time and inclination but not spirits. I try to keep melancholy thoughts out of my mind, but when writing home I can't.

—R. B. H."

September 29, 1842, Dayton, Ohio, Mass Meeting for Henry Clay

The group of statesmen following the Founding Fathers who took over the political imagination of the United States included the Great Triumvirate of Daniel Webster, John Calhoun, and Henry Clay. None were fortunate enough to be elected president, though all repeatedly tried.

Hayes was fond of both Webster and Clay. As a child, Hayes would entertain visitors to his Mother's home by reciting Webster's speeches, including "The Second Reply to Hayne." Later, while attending Harvard, Hayes was privileged to witness in person Webster ratifying the nomination of Henry Clay for president.

Born in 1777 in Kentucky, Clay ran for president five times, including twice on the Whig ticket. Known for his skill in establishing compromise, Clay held many admirers in his wake, and attracted large crowds wherever he spoke.

One such occasion brought Henry Clay to Dayton, Ohio, in the autumn of 1842. The speech took place between Clay's losses of the Whig Party's nomination for president in 1840 to eventual winner William Henry Harrison, and before the 1844 election which Clay lost to James Knox Polk.

Within the audience of 200,000 people that evening in Dayton (according to a sympathetic Whig newspaper), a nineteen-year-old Rutherford Hayes listened intently.

After the speech, Hayes achieved the thrill of a lifetime when he stopped by the house where Clay was relaxing and spoke with him. Another guest, Alfred Kelley of local Republican prominence, remarked to Clay that he had tired himself out by speaking so long, the sixty-five-year-old Clay dismissed the notion saying, "attribute this indiscretion of which you speak to my youth and inexperience."

Perhaps the line Ronald Reagan used in 1984 to dismiss opposing candidate Walter Mondale was an echo of Clay?

Clay would pass away in 1852, long before Hayes would begin his political career. But for an evening, Hayes was face-to-face with the great statesman, on even ground with the man who shaped, through compromise and compassion, the early laws and direction of the United States.

It was a powerful moment for a very young man.

AUGUST 5, 1842, KENYON COLLEGE, VALEDICTORY ADDRESS

Hayes recorded in his diary that the schoolwork at Norwalk bored him. His promise at Middletown was better, and even though his term at Kenyon College began with a rather dry refute of his teachers, Hayes became dedicated to his studies and thrived. On March 15, 1842, Sophia received the following appraisal of her son's education from Mr. S. J. Johnson, a member of the Kenyon College Faculty:

"It becomes my duty, at the close of the present college term, to communicate to you the standing of your son, R. B. Hayes, and I am happy to say that in his studies he has evinced the possession of intellectual powers of a superior order. For strength of mind, clearness of perception, soundness of judgment, he is surpassed by none among us. In all his studies he has attained the highest grade.

In the opinion of all who know him, he bids fair to became a bright ornament to society."

—Mr. S. J. Johnson

In 1842, Valedictorians were elected by the faculty, rather than ranked by their grade point average. Hayes won the esteem of his professors through hard work, dedication to his studies, and a self-esteem which he based on confidence, not arrogance.

As Hayes entered the senior class in November of 1841, he wrote what could have been his valedictory address:

"November 7, 1841—I am now a member of the senior class. Only one short year remains before the frail bark of my destiny will be tossing on the stormy waves of an untried sea. What will be its fate in the voyage of life depends much on the exertions I am now making. I know I have not the natural genius to force my way to eminence, but if I listen to the promptings of ambition, 'the magic of mind' I must have; and since I cannot trust to inspiration, I can only acquire it by 'midnight toil' and 'holy emulation.'

My lofty aspirations I cannot conceal even from myself; my bosom heaves with the thought; they are part of myself, so wrought into my very soul that I cannot escape their power if I would. As far back as memory can carry me, the desire of fame was uppermost in my thoughts. But I never desired other than honorable distinction, and before I would 'be damned to eternal fame,' I would descend to my grave unknown. The reputation which I desire is not that momentary eminence which is gained without merit and lost without regret. Give me the popularity which runs after, not that which is sought for. For honest merit to succeed amid the tricks and intrigues which are now so lamentably common, I know is difficult; but the honor of success is increased by the obstacles which are to be surmounted. Let me triumph as a man or not at all.

Defeat without disgrace can be borne, but laurels which are not deserved sit like a crown of thorns on the head of their possessor. It is indeed far better to deserve honors without having them than to have them without deserving them. Obscurity is an honor to the man who has failed in 'the pursuit of noble ends by noble means.' He can walk proudly forth before the face of nature and be conscious that he has not disgraced the image of his God. Although neglected and perhaps despised by his fellows, there is a monitor within whose approving smiles are more valuable than the plaudits of millions. The first sits upon her seat, unalterable as the sun in its course; the other is more fitful than a summer's breeze. If an honorable man gains the applause of his countrymen, he is richly rewarded, for conscious of his own merit, he feels that it is deserved, and knows that it is substantial because deserved."

—*Hayes, diary*

Every college in the nation should see fit to place these words on every column in their courtyard. "Give me the popularity which runs after, not that which is sought for." For his entire life, Hayes gives real, passionate, meaning to the word, "Duty." The origin of such an honest, sincere, humble creed is rooted in this entry at the start of his senior year at Kenyon.

His valedictory address on August 5, 1842, is an affectionate, personal, and probing recommendation to his friends who remain.

"Fellow Students:

Your situation is very different from that [of] those who will this day go from among you. You have reason to be glad that you are advanced to the rank to which your labors during the part year entitles you—that you are now to have a respite from soil—to return to your homes, to receive the congratulations of friends and enjoy the delights which vacation affords.

We, on the other hand, are about to part forever from scenes endeared to us by many pleasing recollections and fond associations, from companions with whom we have lived in the closest intimacy, and from friends whom we have 'worn in our heart of hearts'...This is the critical period of your lives. So far as human sagacity can forsee, [sic] your present conduct will fix your characters and influence your career for the remainder of your days. In regulating your habits bear this constantly in mind—When deliberating on the propriety of any acts consider first the ultimate result towards which they verge, if you willing that their tendency shall determine your fates, you may soberly perform them, but if you see cause to hesitate be sure that their end is fatal:

You have already heard much, perhaps, too much, of the advantages of College Life. Do not be deceived as to their nature. They confer no distinction, beyond that which superior excellence obtains. On the contrary there is a strong desire among our people to exalt merit when exhibition in self-made men. We cannot complain of this. It is natural and proper. But is [sic] will require greater exertion from us to attain those stations of respectability to which we aspire. Be careful, however, that you do not make too great haste to become learned.

Time is short and the amount of knowledge to be gained, infinite, yet this is a work in which 'too swift arrives as tardy as too slow,' and if in your anxiety to grasp all within your reach, you become superficial, you acquire but little that you can truly call your own, lose the discipline which would enable you to use it promptly and with effect, and deprive yourselves of the power which is required to master what is profound and difficult.

But as it is possible for students to mistake the manner in which they can best secure the benefits of their college course, they are also in danger of being deceived in the kind qualities for which they should labor. Young men are often 'caught by glare' and strive for what is brilliant rather than for what is substantial. We are especially liable to fall into this error, in our public exercises on occasions like the present. We feel it would be vain to attempt to instruct those who favor us with their audience and we therefore endeavor to please by tickling the ear with ornaments of speech and creatures of fancy.

Behold the appeal of the gallant Stark to his little band, when the green hills of Vermont were all gleaming with hostile bayonets, and the flag of England was waving over every peak! His simple words were—'Boys, there's the British and we'll whip them or this night Molly Stark's a widow.'

The phrase was homely but energetic and went straight to the bosoms of the hardy mountaineers around him. It breathes the plain republican spirit of our revolutionary sires—A spirit so honest, and persevering that if we nourish it in its original purity and strength it will bear us safely through the visions and shadows of youth, and sustain us in the dark hours of manhood's adversity—

Heed, we beseech you, those principles of sound morality and learning which will here be taught, and when hereafter Old Kenyon shall count her jewels, may you be recorded among the brightest. Fellow Students—Farewell—"

The Second Inaugural of Lincoln and the only Inaugural of Kennedy are heralded as the greatest speeches of all time. At twenty years of age, Rutherford Hayes uttered words befit a nation of young men (and permit this author to add women) embarking on their college careers. Hayes has, in leaving college, left a singular blueprint for success that the nation's college freshmen in 2016 would be wise to adopt.

The soaring oratory completed, Hayes was back to his humble, jocular self just a few weeks later as he detailed in his diary the past events, "After that came commencement day—that great day for which all other days were made. And it went. And that night I felt of myself all over, and to my astonishment, I found 'twas the same old Rud. Not a single cubit added to my stature; not a hair's-breadth to my girth. If anything, on the contrary, I felt more lank and gaunt than common, much as if a load were off my stomach."

Alas, haven't graduating high school seniors and college seniors through the ages all felt the same thing?

AUGUST 1843, CAMBRIDGE, MASSACHUSETTS, ENTERING HARVARD

"The entrance is steep and difficult, but my chiefest obstacles are within myself. If I knew and could master myself, all other difficulties would vanish. To overcome long-settled habits, one has almost to change 'the stamp of nature;' but bad habits must be changed and good ones formed in their stead, or I shall never find the pearls I seek. Of these matters you shall hear more at another time."

—*Hayes, diary, November 12, 1852*

Hayes spent a year in Columbus studying law in the office of Sparrow and Matthews before he fulfilled his uncle's best wishes and entered Harvard. In the coming term, Hayes would experience world events just a few miles from the birthplace of the American Revolution. Studying in Cambridge, Massachusetts, brought him to the forefront of world affairs. He met former President John Quincy Adams, and, as mentioned previously, heard Daniel Webster ratify the nomination of Henry Clay in 1844, from the audience in Faneuil Hall.

Harvard Law School also allowed Hayes to return to Ohio with a mark on his resume that would only add to the shine of the ornament. He graduated from Harvard in January of 1845, and eagerly embarked on the second stage of his life, a career and a family.

Early career and family...

"Twenty-one! A man in years, a boy in knowledge and wisdom. A third of life gone, and the first rudiments yet to be mastered. But why speak in tones of despondency? Many of those who have been shining lights in the world of learning were as ignorant as I am now when no older than I. Yet they had something in them; aye, and what was the something? Was [it] aught but resolution? And can I not have that? For the future, I'll try to do better, in every sense of the good word, than I ever yet have done."

— *Hayes, diary, October 4, 1843*

January 1, 1845, Cambridge, Massachusetts, Harvard Law School

"This is the beginning of the new year. In two or three weeks I shall leave the Law School and soon after shall begin to live. Heretofore I have been getting ready to live. How much has been left undone, it is of no use to reckon. My labors have been to cultivate and store my mind. This year the character, the whole man, must receive attention. I will strive to become in manners, morals, and feelings a true gentleman.

The rudeness of a student must be laid off, and the quiet, manly deportment of a gentleman put on—not merely to be worn as a garment, but to become by use a part of myself. I believe I know what true gentility, genuine good breeding, is. Let me but live out what is within, and I am vain enough to think that little of what is important would be found wanting."

—*Hayes, diary, January 1, 1845*

Studying the life of Rutherford Hayes, utilizing the immense treasure that is his journal, one can feel him emotionally turn to the next chapter in his life. His graduation from Harvard Law School was yet a few weeks away, but, as was his custom throughout his life, he used the dawn of the new year to stake his claim for the future.

Hayes was ready to meet the challenges ahead.

And there would be many.

Hayes graduated from Harvard Law School on January 17, 1845. With the additional education under his belt, Hayes quickly moved to be reviewed by an Ohio Bar association.

The mechanizations of admission to the Bar, the technical license that allows students of the law to become defenders of the law, are complicated. In the 1840s, the fate of a budding law graduate lay in the hands of a courtly tribunal, consisting of men who had all been through the process before.

Fortunately for Hayes, in 1845, you did not need to be admitted to the Bar at the town or city where you planned to practice. At the urging of Uncle Sardis, Hayes went before the bar in Marietta, Ohio, where the board would contain members already familiar with the Hayes family and whom could serve as accountable cheerleaders of Hayes' stock as a lawyer. It worked.[1]

Hayes at age twenty-three, 1846.

To begin his practice, Hayes left home in Delaware and traveled to a town then called Lower Sandusky, where his uncle Sardis had settled and was happy. The setting, as he explained to Fanny, was perfect:

"I shall enjoy my stay here finely. I can study as much as I wish to and feel independent. The lawyers all treat me kindly and the only ones

I could ever think of dreading are decidedly friendly. I can borrow all the books I want for the present. (I would mend this pen, but my knife is too dull. I left one at Columbus. If it is not found I wish William would send me the best penknife in his shop and charge it to me.)

When I wish to see anybody I can go to Sandusky, Norwalk, or Maumee. I have already made agreeable acquaintances in all the towns in this circuit. I shall spend this week in Lucas County. Judge Lane passed through today. At Sandusky I met a number of my old friends, among others Baker, who was at Cambridge and is now settled at Toledo. So that you perceive I shall not suffer for want of company, although there is no one here of my own age who is fit for a 'trusted cronie.'

...The fact that Lower Sandusky is what it is makes it just the place for me. I have but little competition, taking industry and honesty as among my qualifications, for with one exception (R. P. Buckland) those of our lawyers who are responsible or honest are not industrious, and vice versa."

—*Hayes to Fanny, April 20, 1845*

1.   Hoogenboom, *Rutherford B. Hayes, Warrior & President*, 53.

June 1, 1847, Lower Sandusky, Ohio, War with Mexico

"I have just determined upon a very important step—to go to Mexico, if my health will permit, and in case there is any post within my reach, the duties of which I shall be able to perform. I am induced to this by a mixture of motives. My friends and those whose advice I was bound to listen to, have resolved that I shall leave the office for six months or a year to come, and I can think of no way of spending that time which is half so tolerable as the life of a soldier. If I can enjoy health, I shall be most happy and receive benefit, I am sure. I have no views about war other than those of the best Christians; and my opinion of this war with Mexico is that which is common to the Whigs of the North—Tom Corwin and his admirers of whom I am one. My philosophy has not better principle than that of the old woman who, while she mourned over her neighbor's calamity, was yet rejoiced to be able to witness the conflagration. Whatever doubts I might otherwise have of the morality of this feeling are entirely swamped in the love of enterprise, etc., etc., which I share in common with other young men of my age."

—Hayes, diary, June 1, 1847

The Republic of Texas was annexed into the United States in the waning term of President John Tyler. President James Polk moved quickly to acquire more territory from Mexico, including the territories which now include California and New Mexico. The Mexican government was outraged and refused to speak with an ambassador sent by the new president.

War was inevitable, pitting the two nations against one another, fighting over lands claimed by both governments.

Back in his law office in Lower Sandusky, Hayes became restless. George Washington was his boyhood hero. And he longed to follow in his footsteps on the battlefield. On June 1, he had made up his mind. Unfortunately for Hayes, this decision was met with fierce opposition from his family. All three of his closest and dearest relatives, Mother Sophia, Sister Fanny, and Uncle Sardis disapproved of his plan.

During this same time, as noted in the above diary entry, Hayes was battling a bad cough, enough to lead doctors to suggest his symptoms indicated tuberculosis. They blamed his sedentary lifestyle and advised him to take on, according to biographer Harry Barnard, "an outdoor existence."

Uncle Sardis convinced his nephew to go only if two doctors in Cincinnati reviewed his health and approved the trip. Much to the dismay of Hayes, and unaware Sardis had met with the doctors, he was told the war plan was a huge mistake and that he should not go. Sardis had instructed the doctors to say as much, and Hayes was devastated.

The war would end with the Treaty of Guadalupe Hidalgo in 1848.

It would be another fourteen years before Hayes would see a battlefield. But he would indeed be ready for the challenge.

JULY 6, 1847, DELAWARE, OHIO, MEETING LUCY WEBB

"Between you and I, a little squad of girls have spent a great deal of time and pains in trying to get acquainted with me—calling to see a young married woman at our house and deputizing her to call me in, but I have been so ungallant that they now despair of accomplishing their object. Their messenger wanted me to explain why I was so averse. I first told her that I was no lady's man, but as that wouldn't do I then told her I was engaged to a girl in Columbus, which has relieved me from all trouble. The point now is to find out who my engagee is. This is to be discovered by learning who I write to, but as I don't write to any miss, I think they will not be the wiser from a knowledge of my correspondents."

—*Hayes to Fanny, April 20, 1845*

Twenty-three-year-old men in 2016 might find it difficult to accept that Rutherford Hayes took to telling fibs in order to keep the women off his doorstep, but he did. Hayes scholar Ari Hoogenboom repeatedly refers to the Hayes "luck" and here the same fortune smiles on Hayes in his social circle as it would on the battlefields of western Virginia in two decades.

There is no science with whom one falls in love. There is no equation, no melody, no predetermined duel of the fates that pit this man or that man with this woman and that woman. A boy growing up in

Delaware, Ohio, could just as soon marry a girl growing up in Topeka, Kansas, in 1847, than the girl across the road.

But upon betrothal, one can look back on the happenstance and luck and find nothing short of divine intervention to pairing mates.

Rutherford Hayes met Lucy Webb for the first time at the Sulphur Spring in Delaware, Ohio. Perhaps not luck but, according to his letters, the intervention and encouragement of the mothers of Rud and Lucy created this magic moment. The Sulphur Spring, much the gathering place for young people then as it is now, was thought to have cleansing power in the early nineteenth century. To this day, the spring is held in high regard, most recently undergoing a 'renovation' in 2005 so that more people could be accommodated at its source.

Miss Webb was sixteen years old. The duty Hayes referred to continually in his life would keep him from anything serious with Miss Webb until prudent. Until that time, he would attract and detract from a number of available young women. Luck? Fate? Whichever it may be, the love that would grow between Rutherford and Lucy Hayes is equal in the halls of the White House to that of Abigail and John Adams, Bess and Harry Truman, and Rosalyn and Jimmy Carter.

June 13, 1851, Cincinnati, Ohio, The Proposal

Hayes was twenty-nine years old when he finally decided to make Lucy his wife, and it would be another year and a half before they married. It was Hayes's goal to make his practice profitable before he engaged the vows. Ever the gentleman, providing for Lucy was as important to Hayes as the sanctity of the marriage itself.

He wrote in his diary on January 26, 1852, "Money and reputation have occupied my thoughts the past three weeks, chiefly the former. The latter, I care little about, except the good name which follows every good life. Fame, I care nothing for—positively nothing. Health certainly, brains possibly, is lacking to gain it. The woman I think of often enough, the one with 'the eye that reaches back to the spirit,' whoever she may be, is required to complete all my visionary pictures of quiet bliss hereafter. Money is needed to enjoy the essentials. So gold and love for the future! What a firm! But yet I am prudent."

He does not specifically point out the "woman I think of often enough" is Lucy, but it is probable. On Friday, May 23, he returns in his diary to the topic of Lucy. And again, his entire thought process is worth recording uninterrupted:

"I guess I am a good deal in love with——. (He does not name her.) I have suspected it for some time. It grows on me. Her low sweet voice is very winning, her soft rich eye not often equaled; a heart as true as steel, I know. Miss Clarinda Wright is right. A good heart is a higher quality, a richer possession, than great intellect, especially in a woman. The highest emotion [is] love for our Maker, or for his highest attributes exhibited in his creatures. Well, on that principle L[ucy] is certainly behind no one I have yet seen. Intellect, she has, too, a quick sprightly one, rather than a reflective, profound one. She sees at a glance what others study upon, but will not, perhaps, study out what she is unable to see at a flash. She is a genuine woman, right from instinct and impulse rather than judgment and reflection. It is no use doubting or rolling it over in my thoughts. By George! I am in love with her! So we go. Another bachelor's reverie! Let it work out its own results."

Another month more would pass before he called on her at her home. The day itself did not start out with plans to propose. And without the proposal the day itself might very well have made a significant impact on Hayes' life. On the way to Lucy's house, a horse which must have been spooked charged towards Hayes and another woman walking down the street at the same time. Hayes saved the woman from being trampled by shoving her across the sidewalk. She thanked him and he continued on to Lucy's house. Is it possible this act of chivalry might have encouraged him to act on his surging feelings with Lucy?

Later that evening, as Hayes tells it, he was looking at his love:

"On a sudden the impulse seized me—unthought of, un[pre]meditated, involuntary, and (I was sitting in a rush-bottom rocking-chair in front of her, she on a short sofa) I grasped her hand hastily in my own and with a smile, but earnestly and in quick accents said, 'I love you.' She did not comprehend it; really, no sham; and I repeated [it] more deliberately. She was not startled—no fluttering; but a puzzled expression of pleasure and surprise stole over her fine features. She grew more lovely every breath, returned the pressure of my hand. I knew it was as I wished, but I waited, perhaps repeated (my declaration) again, until she said, 'I must confess, I like you very well.' A queer, soft, lovely tone, it stole to the very heart, and I, without loosing her hand took a seat by her side, and—and the faith was plighted for life!

A quiet, smiling, satisfied silence, broken by an occasional loving word followed. She said, 'I don't know but I am dreaming. I thought I was too light and trifling for you.' I spoke of friends. She said in reply to (my question), 'What would your mother think of her daughter's foolish act?'—'What would your sister think of it?' And so, and so—[Her] brother Joseph came in, and after a short while I went home to dream of it all again and again."

Have we any other narrative of a future president proposing to his wife so filled with sweetness, tenderness, and love as this? Such passion would not diminish from his remarks about Lucy for the rest of his life.

NOVEMBER 26, 1852, EXECUTION YARD,
HAMILTON COUNTY, WITNESS TO A HANGING

The year 1852 brought two significant trials for Rutherford Hayes. Both cases involved murder, and both involved Hayes representing the accused. In the first case, a woman named Nancy Farrer was indicted in the murder of an eight-year-old boy named James Wesley Forest. There were others she allegedly murdered with arsenic, but the heinous act on the young boy was the only crime brought to trial. Hayes concentrated his efforts in the defense on her sanity, and also pulled on the heartstrings of the jury by pointing out Ms. Farrer, if convicted and hanged, would be the first woman to be executed in the State of Ohio.

Hayes lost the trial.

Fortunately, he was able to gain a new trial later by suing by writ of error. In the long slow process of the courts, Nancy Farrers' life was spared for a while longer.

In the meantime, Hayes was assigned to defend another murderer. Hayes assisted with a third case for murder in May of 1852. The murderer was defenseless, and was scheduled to be hanged on November 26, 1852. Just a month before his wedding to Lucy, Hayes witnessed the execution. Seeing the act confirmed his resolve to work even harder to try to save his two defendants, if not from prison, but from death.

Eventually, Hayes argued successfully that Nancy Farrer was of unsound mind and the fate of his other defendant, James Summons, was changed from execution to life in prison.

It is perhaps difficult to understand Hayes working so determinedly to free his clients, at least from the gallows. For the rest of his life, Hayes would recommend and push for strong prison reform, awarding a humanity to prisoners they otherwise could not afford.

Hayes admiration and love for his fiancée overflows in his letters to her:

"Dearest: …So long as that loving heart is true, and it cannot be otherwise, I shall view all you do and say through a medium which makes the rough places smooth and the dark light. But when the thing done is one which pleases me so well as a good letter from you never fails to do, my warmest acknowledgments to you, instead of your apology to me, are what is natural and appropriate…

I think of you constantly, but especially these fine moonlit evenings as I walk the porch in front of this pleasantly shaded farmhouse. I don't just know how I shall get through the summer without seeing you. I suspect I shall have to run down to Chillicothe to see you. I did mean not to do it. I hate going until the railroad is finished. I've said so often I'd not go until it was.

Think of me all pleasant thoughts, as I always do of you, and I will promise to love you ever as I do now. Yours only, ever, R."

It was a long courtship for two purposes. One, Hayes needed to make money and provide for his future wife. But second, Lucy wished to remain with her mother as long as possible in Chillicothe. (Lucy's father died when she was two years old.)

As the winter closed in on Cincinnati in late 1852, the Hayes resolve was tightening and he wished to make his life complete by marrying Lucy. He wrote to Sardis:

Lucy and Rutherford Hayes, 1877.

"Dear Uncle: When I got up this morning I made up my mind that this thing of passing my days as a bachelor was a humbug. The only reason for doing it that I can think of is that I am not making money. Well, I have thought this over and come to the conclusion that I never shall get rich as a bachelor. I doubt if I ever shall as a married man, but I am a-going to take the step.

I am a tolerable lawyer and I can do diverse other things tolerably well. Possibly the stimulus of having others depending on me may sharpen my wits in the way of getting money; but whether or no, I shall fix the day tomorrow before going to Columbus if it can be done, and I think it can."

—Cincinnati, November 20, 1852

Rutherford Hayes and Lucy Webb were married on Thursday, December 30, 1852. They spent the next four weeks at his sister Fanny's house in Columbus.

Hayes recorded the honeymoon was "delightful."[1]

1. Hoogenboom, *Rutherford B. Hayes, Warrior & President*, 86.

JANUARY 1853, COLUMBUS, OHIO, STATE SUPREME COURT

Two different people claimed this particular day as among the most significant in Hayes' life. Hayes himself had exclaimed in his diary on January 7, 1853, that arguing his first case before the Ohio Supreme Court was "the greatest triumph" of his career to that point. The second was a lawyer sitting on the opposing side of the case, Thomas Ewing. Ewing said of Hayes, "That young man will, I predict, make his mark in the state."[1]

Theodore Roosevelt said of his life in the New York State politics, "I rose like a rocket." The same metaphor could be assigned to Hayes inside the Cincinnati courts. Utilizing his natural characteristic of honesty, solid preparation, and effective defense, Hayes was propelled by his peers and the judges from an insignificant case to one of great importance (Farrer) to another whose case he now argued before the Ohio State Supreme Court, '*State of Ohio v. James Summons.*'

According to the court, Summons poisoned his family. According to Hayes, he was an imbecile. The definition of imbecile in the middle of the nineteenth century was much different than the vulgar term it conjures today. Imbeciles, in the vernacular of the 1850s, could not care for themselves. Hayes also concentrated on a fact that the court based its decision on a witness who was, by rule, not cross examined. On this very fact, he was victorious and saved James Summons.[2]

1. Hoogenboom, Rutherford B. Hayes, *Warrior & President*, 87.

2. Hoogenboom, Rutherford B. Hayes, *Warrior & President*, 89.

April, 1853, Fremont, Ohio, First Oral Argument in Federal Court

Sardis had remained in Fremont, and was building a home that would eventually become Rutherford Hayes' Spiegel Grove. There was great interest both with Sardis and with Rutherford concerning Fremont becoming a viable, growing city. And to do that, the city needed a railroad.

In April, 1853, Hayes was asked to provide a brief outlining the City of Fremont's case against the Junction Railroad, who had promised to build a railroad through Fremont to connect Cleveland and Toledo, but were now bent on bridging Sandusky Bay instead.

The case did not go well from the start for Sardis, and by extension the city of Fremont. Hayes wrote to him in May, instead of nephew to uncle, it feels very much like the reverse or perhaps even father to son:

"Dear Uncle: ...Don't lose confidence in humanity. You have, perhaps, had too much hitherto and are now going to the opposite extreme. The men you are now doubtful about were never the best specimens of the race. None of them. It is needful as you are getting along in life that you should not dwell too much on the dark side of things; keep your thoughts on the bright side. You have preserved your cheerfulness in spite of ill health; don't now yield it up to Father Time. The Rome Railroad will do you ten times as much good as the [Sandusky] Bay bridge can do you harm."

—*Cincinnati, May 18, 1853*

After legal maneuvering and the Junction Railroad's merger with another railroad, compromise was settled in Norwalk, Ohio, to assuage the interests of both Fremont, and therefore Uncle Sardis, and the railroads.[1] In what would become a fortunate boon for Fremont, Hayes was selected to defend the city's interest and as a result, plant the seeds of affection for which was sewn a lifelong love affair with the city and its people.

1.   Hoogenboom, Rutherford B. Hayes, *Warrior & President,* 93.

NOVEMBER 4, 1853, CINCINNATI, OHIO, BIRTH OF SON BIRCHARD

"On Friday, the 4th, at 2 P. M., Lucy gave birth to our first child—a son. I hoped, and had a presentiment almost, that the little one would be a boy. How I love Lucy, the mother of my boy! Sweetheart and wife, she had been before, loved tenderly and strongly as such, but the new feeling is more 'home-felt,' quiet, substantial, and satisfying.

For the 'lad' my feeling has yet to grow a great deal. I prize him and rejoiced to have him, and when I take him in my arms begin to feel a father's love and interest, hope and pride, enough to know what the feeling will be if not what it is. I think what is to be his future, his life. How strange a mystery all this is! This to me is the beginning of a new life. A happy one, I believe.

The mother and child are both 'resting' this quiet Sabbath morning. She on our bed, he on the lounge, and I alone with them, awake and musing..."

—*Hayes, diary, November 6, 1853*

There is no chance this author may add or detract from such sweet joy in Hayes announcing the birth of a firstborn son.

APRIL 3, 1855, CINCINNATI, OHIO,
U.S. CIRCUIT COURT, SOUTHERN DISTRICT

Six years yet before the Civil War began, the issue of slavery was at a boiling point. Before Representative Preston Brooks attacked Senator Charles Sumner and nearly killed him in the United States Capitol; before Chief Justice Roger Taney issued his Dred Scott decision which repealed all previous attempts at preventing the spread of slavery into new states, Rutherford Hayes found himself tapped to defend a sixteen-year-old slave girl named Rosetta Armstead.

The story, like everything associated with this dreadful stain on our nation's history, is complicated. Rosetta's master, a clergyman from Kentucky, sent Rosetta to Richmond, Virginia, by railroad under the care of an associate. While they were in Columbus, abolitionists intercepted Rosetta and (unbelievably) set in motion a series of events which led to her freedom. How? They secured a writ of habeas corpus, which is a grand lawyerly term for someone seeking relief from unlawful imprisonment. During this time period, her owner, the clergyman, came to Columbus and simply asked Rosetta if she wanted to be free, or return to Kentucky with him. Rosetta chose freedom and her owner agreed and left.

Unfortunately, her former owner regretted his decision, and decided to come back for Rosetta. She was arrested until the outcome was administered.

At the end of the trial, Hayes was chosen to present the final argument. In the opinion of all present, Hayes performed admirably and Rosetta was set free, again.

This day could only enhance Hayes's prominence, and the question of how, or why, this case did not become a rallying cry for the abolitionists, or the slaveholders is unknown, and perhaps not pertinent to this book. That Hayes was triumphant in securing freedom for a former slave without bloodshed is a high point in his legal career.

July 16, 1856, Columbus, Ohio, "And such a sister!"

Almost thirty-four years to the day following the death of Rutherford Hayes, Sr., his daughter and the beloved sister of "Rud" was gone. The sickness that had engulfed Fanny Hayes Platt years earlier had not completely let go its grip on the young woman. She lost her twin daughters one month prior to her death and succumbed herself on July 16, 1856.

Hayes was devastated:

"July, 1856—My dear only sister, my beloved Fanny, is dead! The dearest friend of childhood, the affectionate adviser, the confidante of all my life, the one I loved best, is gone; alas! never again to be seen on earth. Oh, how we shall always mourn her loss! How we shall lament her absence at every family meeting.

The pride of us all, the charm of every circle, and my own particular loss. It was not a sudden, unexpected blow. We have felt anxious about her several months. On the 16th of June she gave birth to twins—both dead or nearly so when born. Fanny barely survived. Her fine constitution alone enabled her to rally after the severest and most exhausting trial which her experienced physicians had ever seen. She remained in a critical situation, sometimes apparently recovering and again sinking, until her death on the 16th of July, Wednesday evening, about 10 o'clock.

I went up on the first of July and remained until the 10th, when hoping that she was gaining I returned home. She was too weak and low to talk much, but all her finest traits of character were shown in all she said and did up to the very last moment. She never complained, was patient and cheerful always; looked forward to the great change hopefully and with entire confidence that she would meet in Heaven the dear loved ones who had gone before her—her father and Willie—and that there she would soon be joined by the dear friends she was leaving behind. I observed no desire for the ordinary devotions of Christians, and yet she once or twice referred to her Saviour and her desire and expectation of seeing Him.

Once when she supposed she was dying we all gathered around her and brought in her children. She spoke a few kind words to all and spoke of the absent. Turning to me, with her sweetest smile, those beautiful blue eyes, she said: 'Oh, dear Lucy and the boys, how I wish I could see them again but I never shall;' and again: 'Dear Lucy and the boys, how I wish I had talked more about them.' She spoke of Mrs. Wasson and Sophia, and said: 'Dear Uncle, and so many kind, kind friends.' When I brought in little Ruddy, she put her hands lovingly on his pretty fat arms, shoulders, and cheeks, saying: 'Dear boy—sweet child,' and smiled oh, so lovingly. I held one of her hands rubbing it gently. Little Ruddy observing it took the other and rubbed it smiling happily. Fanny said: 'I am going this time.' Little Ruddy spoke up: 'Where are you going, mother?' She replied: 'To Heaven, up to Heaven, I hope, where we shall soon all meet again.'"

—Hayes, diary

Almost a year later, in his diary, Hayes was still bereaved:

"She loved me as an only sister loves a brother whom she imagines almost perfect, and I loved her as an only brother loves a sister who is perfect. Dear, dear Fanny! Let me be just and truthful, wise and pure and good for thy sake! How often I think of her. I read of the death of any one worthy of love and she is in my thoughts. I see, but all things high and holy remind me of her."

For the remainder of his life, Hayes would mention his sister during the happy times and achievements with the same sense of melancholy and longing as he shares above. Her loss was felt deep in his soul, and her memory was never far from his mind.

November 4, 1856, Cincinnati, Ohio, Fremont Defeated

When the Republican Party was formed in 1854–55, Rutherford Hayes participated in its founding in Ohio. The convention was held in Cincinnati, and after Hayes gained fame as a criminal defense attorney, and specifically following his successful argument for the release of Rosetta Armstead, Hayes was a natural choice to be among the founders.

According to Hoogenboom, Hayes was a reluctant participant. An ardent Whig and faithful student of Daniel Webster and Henry Clay, Hayes believed in the platform of the party, but was slow to warm to its waters.

This is not surprising, as Hayes was not often swept away by emotion or peer pressure.

The Republicans, however, in 1856, nominated a man held in high regard by Hayes. General Charles Fremont was not only the first Republican candidate for president, he was the choice of the people of Lower Sandusky when the city needed a popular name from which to distinguish themselves from the other Sanduskys in Ohio.

When Fremont was nominated by the fledgling Republican Party for president in 1856, Hayes was all in. He spoke almost every night for Fremont and, despite Fremont's loss, felt very good about the outcome of the election. Though defeated, Hayes believed their strong showing disabled the Buchanan Democrats, "do not crow over much."

The election had won Hayes over. "However fares the cause," he said on November 2, 1856, before the election, "I am enlisted for the war."

Hayes interest in politics, and the presidency, has two high water marks: his boyish joy at the election of William Henry Harrison in 1840, and his mature understanding and acceptance of defeat in 1856. Both emotions would serve him well in the coming storms of his own political career.

DECEMBER 8, 1858, CINCINNATI, OHIO, APPOINTED CITY SOLICITOR

By the end of 1858, Hayes was well respected in Cincinnati. When a vacancy occurred in the position of City Solicitor, the individual who handles all legal business for the city, Hayes was nominated and elected by the city council. One Democrat, one-very-much-needed Democrat, broke party lines and voted for Hayes securing his election over eleven other foes.

Although it was an appointment, it was his first election. The political career of Rutherford Hayes had begun.

APRIL 4, 1859, CINCINNATI, OHIO, ELECTED SOLICITOR

Hayes won his first election to retain his seat as Solicitor on April 4, 1859. He wrote to his mother the following day:

"Dear Mother: I hope you are not cast down about the election here. It will, I hope, not prove my ruin. Tell William our treasurer got in by about four hundred majority; our mayor has nineteen hundred majority; I have twenty-two hundred.

A good time for unpopular men when the majorities are so great. Lucy and all very well.

Affectionately,

R. B. Hayes"

"It will, I hope, not prove my ruin." That sentence, albeit written to his mother, symbolizes so much of the legacy of Rutherford Birchard Hayes. Believe it or not, politics then was as "vulgar" as it is today, with mudslinging, back door deals and dirty money circulating without regard to party, state, or office. Hayes was stepping into the pit with hesitation. His duty was to serve the people of Cincinnati, but not at the betrayal of his honor.

The position of Solicitor also brought with it the potential for bribery and scandal, none of which ever even approached Rutherford Hayes.

He served two successful years as Solicitor, unblemished by greed.

Abraham Lincoln's election in November of 1860, fired a warning shot into the South. By the time his inaugural train left Springfield, Illinois, seven states in the deep south had seceded. As the train rolled along to Indianapolis, Indiana, a group of city statesmen in Cincinnati made plans to meet him there at the Indiana capitol and accompany him back to their home town. With them, was Rutherford Hayes and his wife Lucy.

The purpose of the inaugural train was to allow the people in the country to meet their new president, albeit from the back of a train. But another advantage for Lincoln was to meet the leaders and politicians of each of the jurisdictions he stopped. What he and his constantly changing guests did not know was their impression of him, and their love for their country, would be critical in the coming months as Lincoln would call for troops. And the same city leaders and politicians would be charged with appointing officers and enlisting hundreds of thousands of men into service.

Such a plan was not in the making as the train roared into Cincinnati on February 12, 1861, Lincoln's fifty-second birthday. Oddly enough, as enthusiastic as Hayes was for Harrison in 1840 and Fremont in 1856, he was silent on Lincoln. He did not even mention in his diary the fortunate train ride with the president-elect.

He does, however, record his thoughts on Lincoln's gait and bow. In a letter to his cousin Laura Platt in Columbus, he writes:

"Don't let Elinor (a sketch artist) fail to catch Lincoln's awkward look when he bows. It can't be caricatured. It is beyond compare—exceeds caricature. His chin rises, his body breaks in two at the hips—there is a bend of the knees at a queer angle. It's good."

—*Letter to Laura Platt, February 13, 1861*

To be fair to Lincoln, Hayes also relayed his confidence in the president-elect to Laura in the same letter, calling him, "Sound." With an evolving legacy still one hundred fifty years later, perhaps Lincoln would be quite content with that one-word sentiment of himself.

April 1, 1861, Cincinnati, Ohio, "My Little Potato Patch Went Down With the Rest."

Hayes suffered his first defeat as the North reacted to the South's movements toward war. To reflect, Hayes wrote to his uncle:

"Dear Uncle: Before this reaches you, you will no doubt learn that the Union-saving avalanche has overtaken us, and that my little potato patch went down with the rest. To prevent a general break-up of the Fusion, both wings agreed as far as possible, to vote an open ticket without scratching. By the aid of oceans of money and a good deal of sincere patriotism in behalf of Union, the plan was carried out with perfect success. It did not in the least disappoint me.

Now, what to do next and how to begin? My term expires next Monday. I shall keep my eyes open, and meditate making you a short visit before finally settling. I have enough cash on hand, or available, to support me for a year, even if I should fail to get business enough to do it, which I do not anticipate. Nothing unpleasant has occurred in the whole course of the canvass. I am quite as well content as one who has drawn a blank ever is, or can be.

Sincerely,

R. B. Hayes"

—Cincinnati, April 2, 1861

A tidal wave of anti-Republican fervor swept Hayes out of office. His letter to Sardis proves he had indeed not been 'ruined' by politics, as he took the vote of the people in stride.

His question of what to do next would be answered in ten days, when someone, who knows which side, started firing in Charleston Harbor at the site of Fort Sumter.

The Civil War...

"Dear Uncle: We are all for war. The few dissentients have to run like quarter-horses. A great change for two weeks to produce. As the Dutchman said, 'What a beeples.' Poor Anderson! What a chance he threw away.

The Government may overlook or even whitewash it, but the people and history will not let him off so easily. I like it. Anything is better than the state of things we have had the last few months. We shall have nothing but rub-a-dub and rumors for some time to come.

All pretty well. Mother thinks we are to be punished for our sinfulness, and reads the Old Testament vigorously. Mother Webb quietly grieves over it. Lucy enjoys it and wishes she had been in Fort Sumter with a garrison of women. Dr. Joe is for flames, slaughter, and a rising of the slaves. All the boys are soldiers.

Sincerely,

R. B. Hayes"

————— Hayes to Sardis, Cincinnati, April 15, 1861

APRIL 16, 1861, CINCINNATI, OHIO, MASS MEETING

President Lincoln's Inaugural Address on March 4, 1861, eloquently and fervently begged the South to stay in the Union. Fat chance. Off the shores of South Carolina in Charleston Harbor stood Fort Sumter. It is not the purpose of this book to report which side fired first because it is debatable. But cannon fire roared in the harbor on April 12, 1861.

Both sides of the Mason-Dixon Line stirred. On April 15, the president called for 75,000 volunteers. On April 16, a mass meeting was held in Cincinnati. Easily recognizable and two years an elected official, Hayes moved for a resolution "upholding the Union against the rebels in disloyal states." According to the *Cincinnati Intelligencer* printed on April 18:

"...Whatever men or means may be necessary to accomplish that object the patriotic people of the loyal States will promptly and cheerfully furnish.

Resolved, That the citizens of Cincinnati will, to the utmost of their ability, sustain the general Government in maintaining its authority, in enforcing the laws, and in upholding the flag of the Union."

According to Douglas Alan Cohn, author of *The President's First Year*, Lincoln's call for volunteers forced four additional southern states into secession, states that were in current discussions to remain in the Union, and states that would eventually provide half of the total army of the Confederacy. The states of Virginia, Arkansas, North Carolina, and Tennessee continued the domino effect of southern rebellion. In Cincinnati, it was not yet known whether neighboring Kentucky would follow the leader.

Just one month earlier, Hayes mused to his uncle about what he was going to do. Now, he was jotting down notes in his diary about how Cincinnati might be protected from an attack if Kentucky were to secede. He recorded these thoughts in his diary in April, 1861:

"To be ready on the day that Kentucky secedes to take possession of the hills on the Kentucky side which command Cincinnati, or the approaches to it, and prepare to hold them against any force.

a. Regiments ready to cross on short notice with arms; ammunition, provisions, tools, etc., for entrenching; cannon, boats, and all essentials.

b. Cut off telegraphic communication south from Covington & Newport.

c. Also railroad communication.

d. Take all boats; fortify all hills, etc.

e. The prevention of raids to rob banks, etc.

f. Spies to Frankfort with passwords for dispatches, etc."

George Washington would have been proud. In the coming days, Hayes will leap from the pages of a diary to the fields of battle.

April 21, 1861, Sunday, Cincinnati, Ohio,
Elected Captain of the Burnet Rifles

In Cincinnati, Hayes was a proud member of the Literary Club, a group of gentlemen meeting monthly with like-minded individuals much the same way as Masons, Eagles, and others meet today. Shortly after Fort Sumter, the group formed a Rifle Club to practice and prepare, to protect Cincinnati or to volunteer themselves for the effort. Naturally, the group elected Hayes Captain. With each passing day, the echo of 'what to do' sounded repeatedly inside him.

The talk of war consumed the city. Hayes wrote the following his college friend from Texas, Guy Bryan:

"We shall, of course, not agree about the war. We shall, I am sure, remain friends. There are good points about all such wars. People forget self. The virtues of magnanimity, courage, patriotism, etc., etc., are called into life. People are more generous, more sympathetic, better, than when engaged in the more selfish pursuits of peace. The same exhibition of virtue is witnessed on your side. May there be as much of this, the better side of war, enjoyed on both sides, and as little of the horrors of war suffered, as possible, and may we soon have an honorable and enduring peace!

P.S. My eldest thinks God will be sorely puzzled what to do. He hears prayers for our side at church, and his grandmother tells him that there are good people praying for the other side, and he asks: "How can He answer the prayers of both?"

—*Hayes to friend Guy Bryan of Texas, May 8, 1861*

Through the looking glass of the twenty-first century, the above letter to Guy Bryan is difficult to accept. That there are "good points" about all wars is certainly true, but the human sacrifice needed to fulfill those rewards are no longer deposits Americans are willing to make. But Hayes is right. War points us all in the same direction, uniting a vast array of class, creed, and races on one single purpose.

"Judge Matthews and I have agreed to go into the service for the war, if possible into the same regiment. I spoke my feelings to him, which he said were his also, viz., that this was a just and necessary war and that it demanded the whole power of the country; that I would prefer to go into it if I knew I was to die or be killed in the course of it, than to live through and after it without taking any part in it."

—Hayes, diary

Fourteen years previously, doctors had told Hayes he was not fit for service, and he should concentrate on building up his body. He had done

just that. Now, his mind, body and soul were "all for war" and all for Union. Remember, Hayes was thirty-eight years old. His age, family, and contacts could have provided honorable reasons not to join the effort. But duty called, and Rutherford Hayes never left that call unanswered.

Instead of pulling strings to keep him out of the war, Hayes put in motion the necessary steps for a volunteer officer's commission. Hayes was sworn in on June 12, 1861, at Camp Chase near

Hayes during Civil War era.

Columbus. He began his service with the rank of Major with the 23rd Regiment of the Ohio Volunteers.

"Colonel Rosecrans and Matthews, having gone to Cincinnati, and Colonel King to Dayton, I am left in command of camp, some twenty-five hundred to three thousand men—an odd position for a novice, so ignorant of all military things. All matters of discretion, of common judgment, I get along with easily, but I was for an instant puzzled when a captain in the Twenty-fourth, of West Point education, asked me formally, as I sat in tent, for his orders for the day, he being officer of the day. Acting on my motto, 'When you don't know what to say, say nothing,' I merely remarked that I thought of nothing requiring special attention; that if anything was wanted out of the usual routine I would let him know."

—Hayes, diary, June 16, 1861

Perhaps other men would have taken advantage of the situation to prove their strength, their worth, or their superiority over other officers. Hayes did not. A man approaching forty years of age as Hayes was during this predicament, perhaps knows his place—and not his place. A much younger man, even a much younger Hayes, might have at least walked through the barracks with his chest out. This author thinks not. From the very start of his life, Hayes adopted a quiet, reserved, conscious quality of knowing exactly when to move forward, step back, and remain.

The men appreciated it. Weeks later, a young private named William McKinley recalled the difference between Hayes and another officer during a crisis with the outdated weapons issued the volunteers.

The United States was not prepared for war in 1861, and the weapons revealed the fact. The men of the 23rd looked disgustedly at their 'arms' and, according to McKinley, deserved better.[1] Hayes' good friend and fellow officer, Lieutenant Colonel Stanley Matthews, took to the extreme and informed his men anyone who dared refuse the old weapons would be killed.[2] Hayes, on the other hand, traveled tent to tent and reasoned with his men. According to McKinley, he was masterful in the moment. "He said that many of the most decisive battles of history had been won with the rudest weapons. At Lexington and Bunker Hill and many other engagements of the Revolution, our forefathers had triumphed over the well-equipped English armies with the very poorest firearms."[2]

Hayes spent time with the men, explained all the possible reasons for the outdated weapons, and won over their support. McKinley later described Hayes with this powerful statement: He "was so generous and his relations with his men were so kind, and yet always dignified, that he won my heart almost from the start…From that moment our confidence in our leader never wavered."[3]

Once again, the quiet reserve and kind-heartedness of Rutherford Hayes served him well. Fortunately, Hayes won over his men at Camp Chase, deep in the center of Ohio and far from the cannon fire of an actual war. He would call on such loyalty repeatedly over the next four years.

1. Perry, James M., *Touched With Fire, Five Presidents and the Civil War Battles that Made Them*, (New York City, Public Affairs™, 2003), 131

2. Perry, *Touched With Fire, Five Presidents and the Civil War Battles that Made Them*, 132.

3. Perry, *Touched With Fire, Five Presidents and the Civil War Battles that Made Them*, 133.

July 24–25, 1861, Camp Chase, Ohio, Marching to War

"Just received news of a dreadful defeat at Manassas, or beyond Centreville. General McDowell's column pushed on after some successes, were met apparently by fresh troops, checked, driven back, utterly routed! What a calamity! Will not the secession fever sweep over the border States, driving out Kentucky, Missouri, (Baltimore) Maryland, etc., etc.? Is not Washington in danger? I have feared a too hasty pushing on of McDowell's column into ground where the Rebels have camped and scouted and entrenched themselves for months.

My brother-in-law, as surgeon, is with the Second Ohio Regiment in advance, and is doubtless among those in the worst position. But private anxieties are all swallowed up in the general public calamity. God grant that it is exaggerated!

Our regiments are now likely, I think, to be speedily needed at Washington or elsewhere. I am ready to do my duty, promptly and cheerfully. Would that I had the military knowledge and experience which one ought to have to be useful in my position! I will do my best, my utmost in all ways to promote the efficiency of our regiment. It is henceforth a serious business."

—*Hayes, diary, July 22*

There is none such bittersweet moment than that of a soldier leaving for war, even at age thirty-eight. As significant as the day he left is the day before, which he spent visiting Columbus and his wife. Lucy's sadness at the departing surprised him. Hayes recorded in his diary on July 26, "Lucy showed more emotion at my departure than she has hitherto exhibited. She wanted to spend my last night with me in Camp Chase." Hayes agreed with Lucy and they spent the final night at camp together. The next morning, Lucy traveled back to Columbus to bring her mother to camp, no doubt so she was not standing there alone as Hayes marched away.

There were already 4,730 casualties in the Civil War the moment the 23rd Regiment of Ohio Volunteers marched to the rail cars to take them to Clarksburg, Virginia. (It would not become West Virginia until June 1863). The volunteers had heard and read the reports from the Union disaster at Manassas. They were, as Hayes was, in one moment leaving comfort for what was certain death. Hayes had bravely announced he would rather die in battle than sit it out, and now those words, along with the loving but sad faces of his wife and mother-in-law watching him, rang in his head.

Hayes embarked with his men on July 25, 1861. The scene of the departure is described emotionally by Hayes:

"I marched in with the men afoot; a gallant show they made as they marched up High Street to the depot. Lucy and Mother Webb remained several hours until we left. I saw them watching me as I stood on the platform at the rear of the last car as long as they could see me. Their eyes swam. I kept my emotion under control enough not to melt into tears. —A pleasant ride to Bellaire; staid in the cars all night."

For a short month, Hayes told his men where to stand, where to sit, when to get up, and what to do. As the cars rumbled over the rails through southern Ohio and beyond, he was well aware it was all different. His men would stand in the line of fire, they would sit on muddy fields and in cold tents. They would get up under darkness. And their task now was to fight.

Hayes was on the last train as they pulled out. He recorded he stood on the platform "as long as they could see me" but failed to point out also, it was as long as he could see them, and specifically Lucy, too.

September 11, 1861, Ferry, Virginia, Mettle tested

"This is the land of blackberries. We are a great, grown-up, armed blackberry party and we gather untold quantities. Here there are nearly as many Secessionists as Union men; the women avow it openly because they are safe in doing so, but the men are merely sour and suspicious and silent…

Men are at work ditching around my tent preparatory to a thunder-shower which is hanging over the mountain west of us. One of them I hear saying to his comrade: 'This is the first time I ever used a spade and I don't like it too well.'"

—*Hayes, diary, July 30, 1861, Weston, Virginia*

There are two histories of the Civil War. On one hand, there is what actually happened, a historical record which cannot be argued. Then there is the moment-by-moment account, letter-by-hand-written-letter, of what soldiers *thought* was going to happen. As communicating by mail increased exponentially in 1861 with hundreds of thousands of people writing letters to their husbands, sons, and brothers on the battlefields, the soldiers responded with accurate and often inaccurate assumptions of what was going to happen next. Add to the literary fray newspapers, with both Republican and Democratic sides to advance, officers in the war had to concentrate solely on what their superior officers,' and the headquarters in Washington, DC, had to say.

"Our news is that Wise has continued his retreat burning the bridges after him. This confirms our suspicions as to his abandoning all west of the mountains. There is, however, a report from the East that General Lee is to be sent out here to look after General Rosecrans, with a considerable force. I do not believe it, but if so, we shall have lively times."

—*Hayes to Sardis, July 30, 1861*

The Union Army had suffered a devastating defeat at the Battle of Manassas in Virginia in July, the result of which had caused Hayes and his men to be moved shortly thereafter. The Union could not afford another setback. As August turned to September in the hills of western

Virginia, the news that Lee was on his way reinforced the stark truth to the Ohio 23rd that wherewith Lee came the war.

'He' was not 'Lee' but Confederate Brigadier General John B. Floyd. Floyd surprised and pushed the 7th Ohio Infantry away from Carnifex Ferry and camped on a local farmhouse. Beyond Carnifex Ferry lay the entire Kanawha Valley and the west Virginia theater. The situation was bleak.

The 23rd Regiment of Ohio Volunteers reported to forty-two-year-old Brigadier General William Rosecrans. Rosecrans knew Carnifex Ferry was the first jewel in the crown of what was west Virginia, so he moved three brigades to push back Floyd.

Among them, Rutherford Hayes.

On Sunday evening, August 18, he wrote to Lucy:

"Since writing the above we have received word that the enemy in force is coming towards us through the mountains to the southeast, and have been ordered to prepare three days' rations and to be ready to march at a moment's notice to attack the enemy. I am all ready...

It will be a stirring time if we go, and the result of it all by no means clear. I feel no apprehension—no presentiment of evil, but at any rate you know how I love you and the dear boys and Grandma and all will take care that I am not forgotten. You will know by telegraph long before this reaches you what comes of the anticipated movements. I suspect we are misinformed. At any rate, good-bye, darling. Kisses for all.

Affectionately, R."

Although Hayes mused they were "misinformed," they were not. On September 10, Hayes moved into position with his men. The description of this battle is best left to the man who was there and whose pen moves with dramatic wit and humility.

He recorded in his diary,

"On Tuesday, September 10, Marched seventeen miles, drove enemies' pickets out of Summersville, followed nine miles to Gauley river. Enemy entrenched on a hill, high, steep, and hidden by bushes, three to six thousand strong. We get ready to attack.

First Brigade led the attack. We stood near half an hour listening to the heavy cannon and musketry, then were called to form in line of battle. My feelings were not different from what I have often felt before beginning an important lawsuit...

Finally our turn came. I was told to take four companies and follow one of General Rosecrans' staff. I promptly called off Seventh, Eighth, Ninth, and Tenth companies. We marched over a hill and through a cornfield; the staff officer and myself leading on, until we reached the brow of a high hill overlooking the Gauley River and perhaps three-quarters of a mile from the entrenchments of the enemy. He [the officer] then said to me that I was to be on the extreme left of our line and to march forward guided by the enemy's guns, that he had no special orders to give, that I was an officer and must use my own judgment. He never had been over the ground I was to pass over; thought the enemy might retreat that way.

I marched to the wood; found it a dense laurel thicket on the side of a steep hill, rocky and cavernous; at the bottom a ravine and river and up the opposite hill seemed to be the enemy. I formed the four companies into order of battle, told them to keep together and follow me; in case of separation to push forward in the direction of the declining sun and when the firing could be heard to be guided by it. I handed my horse to one of the unarmed musicians, and drawing my sword crept, pushed, and struggled rapidly down the hill. When I reached the bottom but four or five of Company K (Captain Howard) were in sight. Soon men of Captain Zimmerman's came up and soon I gathered the major part of the four companies. I had sent Captain Woodward and twenty scouts or skirmishers ahead; they were among the unseen.

By this time it was getting late. I formed a line again extending from the river up the hill and facing towards the enemy, as we supposed. The firing had ceased except scattered shots. We pushed slowly up, our right up hill, where I was soon encountered the Twenty-eighth—lost. Had a laugh and greeting with Markbreit who was on the left of the Twenty-eighth (he was my partner). The head of my column was near enough to be fired on. Two were wounded, others hit; none seriously hurt. The face of the hill on which the enemy was posted was towards precipitous rock. We could only reach them by moving to the right in front of the Twenty-eighth, Forty-seventh, and Thirteenth.

I have heard nothing clear or definite of the position, either of the enemy or ourselves…I got up nearer than anybody except the Tenth and Twelfth but was down a steep hill or precipice and concealed. Some of my men bore to the right and pushing in front of the Twenty-eighth and Forty-seventh mixed with the Thirteenth. It soon got dark; all firing ceased. I drew off single file, Captain Sperry leading; got up the hill just at complete dark; found messengers ordering us to return to the rest of our regiment, on the extreme right. Some thirty of my men were missing—Captain Woodward, Lieutenant Rice, etc., etc.

I left ten sentinels along the brow of the hill to direct them where to find us. The greater part soon overtook us. We marched through lost fragments of regiments—Germans mostly, some Irish, talking of the slaughter, until we got into an old field near our regiment. There we waited. Nobody seemed nervous or anxious—all wishing for light. Talked with McCook who criticized the orders, but was in good temper; had lost three horses. Finally found our regiment and all marched off to bivouac. In the morning great cheering near the fort. Enemy had run away in a panic by a road over the hill back of their works, leaving flag, etc."

Rutherford Hayes had played a critical role in why those Rebels were running. Brave, unrelenting and confident, Hayes moved his men forward under fire for the first time. And he would be commended for it in due course.

SEPTEMBER 1861, SOUTH OF SUMMERSVILLE,
[WEST] VIRGINIA, APPOINTED JUDGE ADVOCATE

"September 19, 1861,

Dearest: I have thus far been the sole judge advocate also of this army; so I am very busy. We tried three cases yesterday. It is a laborious and painful business. And after writing so much I would not write you but for my anxiety to have you know how much I think of and love you. Love and kisses to all the boys."

After the war, Hayes would most likely not look back on his assignment as judge advocate with any kind of relish as an important day in his life, mentioning in the same letter as above to Lucy, "It is not altogether agreeable."[1] However, it bears witness to the fact his superiors felt he was a fair and just arbitrator, both from his legal reputation in Cincinnati and also his respectable command on the battlefield. Although he warmed to the position as it allowed him to travel and there was a potential for visiting home, he must have privately lobbied to be back with his men.

He was not judge advocate for very long.

DECEMBER 21, 1861, CINCINNATI, OHIO, BIRTH OF SON, JOSEPH

Lucy gave birth to their fourth son while her husband was at war. The absence pained both Hayes and Lucy. On the father's side, perhaps it drove him harder, more determined than ever to do all he could to assure a Union victory and even more so, assure a return trip home to his family.

"Queer world! We fret our little hour, are happy and pass away. Away! Where to? 'This longing after immortality! These thoughts that wander through eternity!' I have been and am an unbeliever of all these sacred verities. But will I not take refuge in the faith of my fathers at last?

Are we not all impelled to this? The great abyss, the unknown future—are we not happier if we give ourselves up to some settled faith? Can we feel safe without it? Am I not more and more carried along, drifted, towards surrendering to the best religion the world has yet produced?

It seems so. In this business, as I ride through the glorious scenery this loveliest season of the year, my thoughts float away beyond this wretched war and all its belongings. Some, yes many, glorious things, as well as all that is not so, [impress me]; and [I] think of the closing years on the down-hill side of life, and picture myself a Christian, sincere, humble, devoted, as conscientious in that as I am now in this—not more so.

My belief in this war is as deep as any faith can be; —but thitherward I drift. I see it and am glad."

—*Hayes, October 29, 1861*

November 2, 1861, Sewell Mountain,
Promoted to Lieutenant Colonel

"Dear L: We are in the midst of a very cold rain-storm; not farther south than Lexington or Danville and on the top of a high hill or small mountain. Rain for fifteen hours; getting colder and colder, and still raining. In leaky tents, with worn out blankets, insufficient socks and shoes, many without over coats. This is no joke. I am living with McCook in a good tent, as well provided as anybody in camp; better than either General Cox or Rosecrans.

I write this in General Cox's tent. He sits on one cot reading, or trying to read, or pretending to read, Dickens' new novel, *Great Expectations*."

—*Hayes to Lucy, September 27, 1861*

Buried in between troop movements and battle stories and even the harsh conditions the soldiers (and officers) endured in the Civil War is a gem of an observation from Hayes. He liked General Rosecrans, and as he wrote to his dear wife, imagine him glancing up every now and then contemplating whether the General was "reading," "trying to read," or just "pretending to read" is a marvelously human moment in the middle of a dreadfully wicked war.

Hayes returned to his men in November of 1861, after his good friend Colonel Matthews was also promoted. On November 2, he allowed himself a private boast to his wife, "I confess to the weakness of preferring (as I must hereafter always be called by some title) to be called Colonel to being styled Major."

He also preferred to be back with his men. Undoubtedly, they preferred the same.

May 10, 1862, Giles Court House, Battle of Pearisburg

Hayes had spent his first winter in the war at Fayetteville, (West) Virginia. The new Lieutenant Colonel, like Washington at Valley Forge, stayed with his regiment rather than returning home or to quarter in the nearest city. It was another reason Hayes was held high in the hearts of his men.

He did, however, make it home in February to see his family and his new son, Joseph, born December 21, 1861.

The rumor mill was still in fine whack by the time the spring rains moved out and loosened the tight grip of Winter Quarters. For the men of the 23rd, it was a long rest, as they did not set out for a spring campaign until late April, 1862. Hayes and his men marched to the town of Princeton which had been left burning by retreating Rebels. With a desire to capture supplies, Hayes continued to move forward until ordered to stop by commanding officer (and Rosecrans replacement Colonel Scammon) at Giles Court House in a town Hayes repeatedly called "Parisburg." The actual name is spelled Pearisburg. You can assume the local pronunciation from Hayes spelling.

Hayes was in a desperate situation, and he knew it. His diary reveals a man beginning to bend, but not break:

"Princeton, May 6, 1862—I have been rather anxious today. We heard from contrabands and others that the Narrows [of New River] was deserted except by a small guard for property and tents. Major Comly with Companies H, I, and K and Captain Gilmore's Cavalry was dispatched to the point eighteen to twenty-two miles distant. No tidings yet, although a courier ought to have reached here before this time if they and he traveled rapidly. I suggested that if necessary to secure property they go to Giles Town."

"Parisburg, [Pearisburg], May 9, Friday—A lovely day—No reinforcements yet; have asked for them in repeated dispatches. Strange. I shall be vigilant. Have planned the fight if it is to be done in the houses at night, and the retreat to the Narrows, if in daylight with artillery against us. The town can't be held if we are attacked with artillery. Shameful! We have rations for thirty days for a brigade and tents and other property."

Hayes was indeed asking repeatedly for reinforcements. He knew his strength, and the strength of the enemy. Finally, he sent the following to Colonel Scammon:

"Camp Number 6, Giles Court House, May 9, 1862, A.M.,

Sir: —Your dispatch of yesterday reached me about 10:30 o'clock P. M. Its suggestions and cautions will be carefully heeded. If in any important respect my reports are defective, I shall be glad to correct the fault. The novelty of my situation and the number and variety of claims upon my attention must be my apology for what may seem negligence. Our men and horses are getting worn-out with guard, picket, and patrol duty, added to the labor of gathering in forage and provisions.

You say nothing of the forward movement having been disapproved, nor of abandoning or reinforcing this point. I infer that we may look for reinforcements today. It is of the utmost importance that we get prompt and large additions to our strength.

The facts are these: Large amounts of forage and provisions which we might have got with a larger force are daily going to the enemy. The enemy is recovering from his panic, is near the railroad and getting reinforcements. He is already stronger than we are, at least double as strong.

But all this you already know from repeated dispatches of mine and I doubt not you are doing all you can to bring up the needed additions to our force."

Still no word about reinforcements, Hayes began to plan for the worst:

"Camp Number 6, Giles Court-House, May 9, 1862, 10:30 (P.M.),

Sir: —You will have to hurry forward reinforcements rapidly—as rapidly as possible—to prevent trouble here. This is not a defensible point without artillery against artillery. No news of a movement by the enemy but one may be expected soon. Shall we return to the Narrows if you can't reinforce?

P.S. —A party the other side of the river is firing on our men collecting forage and provisions."

The Rebels were close. Hayes, not yet a year into his military service and with no official training beyond Camp Chase, had repeatedly called for reinforcements for what he knew by instinct was coming.

Again, the masterful Hayes takes us through the battle:

"Saturday, May 10, 4 P.M.—We were attacked at 4 o'clock this morning. I got up at the first faint streak of light and walked out to see the pickets in the direction of the enemy. As I was walking alone I heard six shots. 'No mistake this time,' I thought.

I hurried back, ordered up my own and the adjutant's horse, called up the men and officers, [and] ordered the cavalry to the front. [I ordered] Captains Drake and Sperry to skirmish before the enemy and keep them back; the rest of the regiment to form in their rear. Led the whole to the front beyond the town; saw the enemy approaching—four regiments or battalions, several pieces of artillery in line of battle approaching.

The artillery soon opened on us. The shell shrieked and burst over heads, the small arms rattled, and the battle was begun. It was soon obvious that we would be outflanked.

We retreated to the next ridge and stood again. The men of the Twenty-third behaved gloriously, the men of Gilmore's Cavalry, ditto; the men of Colonel Paxton's Cavalry, not so well. I was scratched and torn on the knee by a shell or something, doing no serious injury. I felt well all the time. The men behaved so gallantly!

And so we fought our way through town, the people rejoicing at our defeat, and on for six hours until we reached the Narrows, five and one-half miles distant. The time seemed short. I was cheered by Gilmore's

Cavalry at a point about three and one-half miles from Giles Court-house, and we were all in good humor. We had three men killed, a number wounded, none severely, and lost a few prisoners.

In the Narrows we easily checked the pursuit of the enemy and held him back until he got artillery on to the opposite side of New River and shelled us out. Reached here about 1 P.M. safely. A well-ordered retreat which I think was creditable."

There was Hayes, leading his men in retreat, enduring the shock which came from nearly having his knee blown apart, and holding his head high as the townspeople cheered the failure. Though proud of his men and their orderly departure, Hayes seethed at the lost opportunity as well.

In his report to General Scammon on May 11, Hayes ended with this: "It is much to be regretted that reinforcements which I had so frequently and urgently requested could not be sent in time to save Parisburg [Pearisburg], as the loss of position and property is very serious."

Unfortunately, Colonel Scammon had the nerve to ask Hayes to erase that sentence. Hayes did as was asked and recorded on the same report for his personal diary he did it "because he wished it, and I did not want to embarrass him."

Later, in a letter to his wife on May 12, Hayes admitted, "Since writing the foregoing, we have got information which leads me to think it was probably well we were not reinforced. There would not have been enough to hold the position we had against so great a force as the enemy brought against us. You see we were twenty miles from their railroad, and only six to twelve hours from their great armies."

Hayes and his men could have faced slaughter had it not been for his orderly retreat. And if he was reinforced, as Hayes admitted, the battle of Giles Court House could have ranked alongside the bloodier and costlier failures of the North. Hindsight is always 20/20 and war reveals untold counts of 'What ifs' but Hayes was fortunate he made it out of Giles Court House with his leg and his life.

Hayes had acted gallantly in the Battle of Pearisburg, and had also been wounded. Naturally, he looked for a promotion to reflect the gratitude of the Army.

"July 23—Last evening I fell into a train of reflection on the separation of the regiment, so long continued, so unmilitary, and so causeless, with the small prospect of getting relief by promotion or otherwise in the Twenty-third, and as a result pretty much determined to write this morning telling brother William [Platt] that I would like a promotion to a colonelcy in one of the new regiments.

Well, this morning, on the arrival of the mail, I get a dispatch from W. H. Clements that I am appointed colonel of the Seventy-ninth, a regiment to be made up in Hamilton, Warren, and Clinton Counties. Now, shall I accept? It is hard to leave the Twenty-third. I shall never like another regiment so well. Another regiment is not likely to think as much of me. I am puzzled. If I knew I could get a chance for promotion in the Twenty-third in any reasonable time, I would decline the Seventy-ninth. But, then, Colonel Scammon is so queer and crotchety that he is always doing something to push aside his chance for a brigadiership. Well, I will postpone the evil day of decision as long as possible."

Hayes loved the 23rd so much the Colonelcy he long desired came as a bittersweet pill. Through two battles, Hayes became enamored with the bravery of his men and adored them for it. They returned the affection twelvefold. In the end, he would not have to leave his beloved troops.

On July 24, 1862, Colonel Scammon asked Hayes to enter enemy territory to retrieve the family of a Union man. Hayes didn't mind the exercise; it was the way Scammon issued the responsibility that caught his ire:

> "I got a lame, halting permission from Colonel Scammon to go on an errand of mercy over New River into Monroe (County) after the family of Mr. Caldwell, a Union man, who has been kept away from home and persecuted for his loyalty. The colonel says I may go if and if; and warning me of the hazards, etc., etc., shirking all responsibility. It is ridiculous in war to talk this way.
>
> If a thing ought to be done according to the lights we have, let us go and do it, leaving events to take care of themselves. This half-and-half policy; this do-less waiting for certainties before action, is contemptible. I rode to the ferry and arranged for the trip with Major Comly."

Hayes successfully saved the Caldwell family, and took delight in the trip despite its irritating origin, writing on July 26, "A pretty jolly expedition! Horses fell down, men fell down; Caldwell got faint-hearted and wanted to give it up."

The excitement of life in the Army was thrilling for Rutherford Hayes. The next challenge for his men came in early August when nearby Rebel troops, thought to be in much greater number than Hayes had at his disposal, set their sights on a local ferry, a ferry which the men serving under Hayes refused to let them take. The Rebels fired cannons into the banks of the other side, hopeful to push back the Union men and take the ferry. Hayes responded with a rallying cry which should have its own shelf in Civil War lore.

"Camp Green Meadows, August 6, 1862—Called up Companies E, C, and K to go to reinforce the ferry. I sent the band to give them music and told the men: 'Fighting battles is like courting the girls: those who make most pretension and are boldest usually win. So, go ahead, give good hearty yells as you approach the ferry, let the band play; but don't expose yourselves, keep together and keep under cover. It is a bushwhacking fight across the river. Don't expose yourself to show bravery; we know you are all brave,' etc., etc. The men went off in high spirits."

Hayes knew his men. And he knew just what to say and how to say it. Major Comly then burned the ferry and the Rebels and all their raucousness retreated. A small victory in a very large war, nonetheless, but the men and Hayes relished it.

SUNDAY, SEPTEMBER 7, 1862, OUTSIDE WASHINGTON CITY,
THE RENO EXCHANGE

The 23rd of Ohio was reassigned under Major-General Reno in September of 1862. They marched through Georgetown and stopped at Leesborough, now Wheaton, Maryland. According to Hayes' diary, the men, though they were in friendly territory, used the bales of straw and wheat to feed horses or lay down on the rigid stubbles of the field. Hayes did not see anything wrong with it. Reno, naturally perhaps, was incensed.

Hayes described the exchange the evening of September 7 in his diary:

"General Reno began on McMullen's men. He addressed them: 'You damned black sons of bitches.' This he repeated to my men and asked for the colonel. Hearing it, I presented myself and assumed the responsibility, defending the men.

I talked respectfully but firmly; told him we had always taken rails, for example, if needed to cook with; that if required we would pay for them. He denied the right and necessity; said we were in a loyal State, etc., etc. Gradually he softened down.

He asked me my name. I asked his, all respectfully done on my part. He made various observations to which I replied. He expressed opinions on pilfering. I remarked, in reply to some opinion, substantially: 'Well, I trust our generals will exhibit the same energy in dealing with our foes that they do in the treatment of their friends.' He asked me, as if offended, what I meant by that. I replied. 'Nothing—at least, I mean nothing disrespectful to you.' (The fact was, I had a very favorable opinion of the gallantry and skill of General Reno and was most anxious to so act as to gain his good will.)

This was towards the close of the controversy, and as General Reno rode away the men cheered me. I learn that this, coupled with the remark, gave General Reno great offense. He spoke to Colonel Ewing of putting colonels in irons if their men pilfered! Colonel Ewing says the remark 'cut him to the quick,' that he was 'bitter' against me. General Cox and Colonel Scammon (the latter was present) both think I behaved properly in the controversy."

Referring back for a moment to the report Hayes filed on the retreat from Giles Court House, perhaps we can assume, if Hayes had not 'erased' the damning sentence for Colonel Scammon, he (Scammon) might have reacted differently to Hayes on this very point. Hayes would also, in politics, learn that doing what is right to another person often brought favor later down the road.

Interestingly, Hayes, about to turn forty years of age, quickly wrote a letter on September 8 to his Uncle Sardis explaining the entire episode and defending himself, just in case Sardis should happen to read about it in the newspapers, "General Cox, Colonel Scammon, and all the Ohio colonels and troops sustain me fully and justify the cheering, saying the men have the same right to cheer their colonel that they have to cheer General McClellan. I think it will stop where it is, except in the newspapers. Whatever is reported, you may feel safe about the outcome."

It was an important day in Hayes' life, standing up for his men in the face of retribution and backlash from a superior officer.

SEPTEMBER 14, 1862, FREDERICK, MARYLAND, BATTLE AT FOX'S GAP

"Your letter of the 13th August, directed to me Raleigh, etc., I got last night. We shall now get one another's letters in three or four days. I was made happy by your sensible and excellent talk about your feelings. A sense of duty or a deep religious feeling is all that can reconcile one to the condition we are placed in. That you are happy notwithstanding this trial, adds to my appreciation and love and to my happiness. Dearest, you are a treasure to me. I think of you more than you suppose and shall do so more here than in western Virginia. Here I have far less care and responsibility. I am now responsible for very little. The danger may be somewhat greater, though that I think doubtful.

By the by, we hear that Raleigh and our camps in west Virginia were occupied by the enemy soon after we left. No difference. There is one comfort here. If we suffer, it is in the place where the decisive acts are going on. In west Virginia, success or failure was a mere circumstance hardly affecting the general cause...

Well, love to all. Dearest be cheerful and content. It will all be well. Affectionately, R."

—Rutherford to Lucy, September 1, 1862

Hayes underestimated the danger of being in Maryland, but he was also trying to calm his wife who was reading daily reports, though some of them inaccurate, of troop movement, battles, and of course daily casualties. Earlier in the above letter, Hayes appreciated the fact she was keeping her head up, despite constant worry. But in two weeks, Hayes would find himself flat on his back.

The war, the relentless onslaught that turned towns into multi-campus hospitals had come to the men of the 23rd on September 14, 1862. The location—South Mountain.

General George McClellan had intercepted intelligence from General Robert E. Lee reporting Lee was planning a major attack on the Union. To stop him, McClellan had to cross South Mountain.

There were three gaps surrounding the mountain, and all of them would eventually host battles: Crampton's, Fox's, and Turner's. McClellan moved first into Turner's Gap, and he chose Reno's Corps to lead the charge. Reno chose the division led by Jacob Cox, and Cox chose Scammon's Brigade in the front. From McClellan to Reno to Cox to now Scammon, the point of the arrow pointed at Lee's Army was led by the 23rd Regiment of Ohio Volunteers and their commander, Rutherford B. Hayes.

What follows is, as has been this author's custom, the Hayes Diary entry describing the battle. There is no possible angle this author could begin to improve upon this prose:

"September 14, Sunday—Enemy on a spur of Blue Ridge, three and one-half miles west. At 7 A. M. we go out to attack. I am sent with Twenty-third up a mountain path to get around the Rebel right with instructions to attack and take a battery of two guns supposed to be posted there. I asked, 'If I find six guns and a strong support?' Colonel Scammon replies, 'Take them anyhow.'

Went with a guide by the right flank up the hill, Company A deployed in front as skirmishers. Seeing signs of Rebels [I] sent [Company] F to the left and [Company] I to the right as flankers. Started a Rebel picket about 9 A.M. Soon saw from the opposite hill a strong force coming down towards us; formed hastily in the woods; faced by the rear rank (some companies inverted and some out of place) towards the enemy; pushed through bushes and rocks over broken ground towards the enemy; soon received a heavy volley, wounding and killing some.

Hayes during Civil War era.

I feared confusion; exhorted, swore, and threatened.

Men did pretty well. Found we could not stand it long, and ordered an advance. Rushed forward with a yell; enemy gave way. Halted to re-form line; heavy firing resumed.

I soon began to fear we could not stand it, and again ordered a charge; the enemy broke, and we drove them clear out of the woods. Our men halted at a fence near the edge of the woods and kept up a brisk fire upon the enemy, who were sheltering themselves behind stone walls and fences near the top of the hill, beyond a cornfield in front of our position.

Just as I gave the command to charge I felt a stunning blow and found a musket ball had struck my left arm just above the elbow.

Fearing that an artery might be cut, I asked a soldier near me to tie my handkerchief above the wound. I soon felt weak, faint, and sick at the stomach. I laid [lay] down and was pretty comfortable. I was perhaps twenty feet behind the line of my men, and could form a pretty accurate notion of the way the fight was going.

The enemy's fire was occasionally very heavy; balls passed near my face and hit the ground all around me. I could see wounded men staggering or carried to the rear; but I felt sure our men were holding their own. I listened anxiously to hear the approach of reinforcements; wondered they did not come.

I was told there was danger of the enemy flanking us on our left, near where I was lying. I called out to Captain Drake, who was on the left, to let his company wheel backward so as to face the threatened attack. His company fell back perhaps twenty yards, and the whole line gradually followed the example, thus leaving me between our line and the enemy.

Major Comly came along and asked me if it was my intention the whole line should fall back. I told him no, that I merely wanted one or two of the left companies to wheel backward so as to face an enemy said to be coming on our left. I said if the line was now in good position to let it remain and to face the left companies as I intended. This, I suppose, was done.

The firing continued pretty warm for perhaps fifteen or twenty minutes, when it gradually died away on both sides. After a few minutes' silence I began to doubt whether the enemy had disappeared or whether our men had gone farther back. I called out, 'Hallo Twenty-third men, are you going to leave your colonel here for the enemy?'

In an instant a half dozen or more men sprang forward to me, saying, 'Oh no, we will carry you wherever you want us to.' The enemy immediately opened fire on them. Our men replied to them, and soon the battle was raging as hotly as ever. I ordered the men back to cover, telling them they would get me shot and themselves too.

They went back and about this time Lieutenant Jackson came and insisted upon taking me out of the range of the enemy's fire. He took me back to our line and, feeling faint, he laid me down behind a big log and gave me a canteen of water, which tasted so good.

Soon after, the fire having again died away, he took me back up the hill, where my wound was dressed by Dr. Joe. I then walked about half a mile to the house of Widow Kugler. I remained there two or three hours when I was taken with Captain Skiles in an ambulance to Middletown—three and a half miles—where I stopped at Mr. Jacob Rudy's.

I omitted to say that a few moments after I first laid down, seeing something going wrong and feeling a little easier, I got up and began to give directions about things; but after a few moments, getting very weak, I again laid down. While I was lying down I had considerable talk with a wounded [Confederate] soldier lying near me. I gave him messages for my wife and friends in case I should not get up. We were right jolly and friendly; it was by no means an unpleasant experience."

—*Hayes, diary, September 18, 1862*

September 23, 1862, Middletown, Maryland, Lucy Arrives

Hayes was transported to Middletown, Maryland, where he stayed with a family with the last name Rudy. (In a letter to his mother, the jovial spirit remained as he told her the last name and added, "not quite 'Ruddy.'"[1]) He sent three telegrams reporting his wound:

"Frederick, Maryland, September 15, 1862,

To W. A. Platt, Columbus, Ohio,

I am seriously wounded in the left arm above the elbow. The Ohio troops all behaved well. R. B. Hayes"

He sent one to his brother-in-law, one to his friend John Herron, and of course one to his wife.

On September 20, Hayes recorded the following in his diary, "Got a dispatch from Platt. Fear Lucy has not heard of my wound; had hoped to see her today, probably shan't. This hurts me worse than the bullet did."

Tragically, the messenger who sent the telegrams had enough money to send two, which were ordered for the men. Lucy had no idea her husband was wounded until she received a second telegram from Hayes, "I am here. Come to me, I shall not lose my arm."[2]

She came. But tragically and unintentionally, she went to the wrong place. In an earlier letter, Hayes had said he would be at the Kirkwood House in Washington, DC, if he was wounded. Lucy bypassed Fredericktown not knowing her husband was there, then, not finding him in Washington, traveled back to Baltimore and finally reached her husband the evening of September 23.

The reunion, more than a week following his wound, began with a quip from Hayes about the need to see Washington and Baltimore first. Lucy, anxious and nervous and scared herself, took it in loving stride. There is no record of an embrace or the tender sweet moments they spent together thereafter, but this was a day that certainly defined Rutherford Hayes. The march to the railcars at Camp Chase had conjured up images of what may lay ahead. Lucy, home in Chillicothe, needed reassurance from her husband on occasion that he would return safely.

And now here he was, on a bed with a wound that could have caused him to lose his arm. Lucy's fears were realized, and perhaps Hayes himself was relieved he was going to be ok. For now, they were together, and that was all that mattered.

1. RBH to Sophia Hayes, September 15, 1862.

2. Hoogenboom, Ari, *One of the Good Colonels*, (Abilene, Texas, McWhiney Foundation Press, 1999) 56–57.

JUNE 24, 1863, CHARLESTON, WEST VIRGINIA, DEATH OF SON, JOSEPH

With Robert E. Lee marching towards Gettysburg, life in the Kanawha Valley in the West Virginia theater was quiet enough for officer's wives and family to visit their husbands. Lucy and the boys came, too. Surrounded by constant reminders of the death of his soldiers, Hayes and his family were dealt an unbelievable blow in the midst of their happy gathering.

"Camp White [opposite Charleston], West Virginia, June 25, 1863— Last Monday, the 15th, Lucy, Mother Webb, and 'all the boys' came here from Cincinnati on the Market Boy. A few happy days, when little Joseph sickened and died yesterday at noon (12:40).

Poor little darling! A sweet, bright boy, 'looked like his father,' but with large, handsome blue eyes much like Webb's. Teething, dysentery, and brain affected, the diseases. He died without suffering; lay on the table in our room in the Quarrier cottage, surrounded by white roses and buds all the afternoon, and was sent to Cincinnati in care of Corporal Schirmes, Company K, this morning. I have seen so little of him, born since the war, that I do not realize a loss; but his mother, and still more his grandmother, lose their little dear companion, and are very much afflicted."

Hayes was painfully honest about the fact he did not feel the loss, but grieved at the heartbreak of his family. In the middle of the Civil War, surrounded by his immediate family and the boys of the 23rd, he watched the train take his eighteen-month-old third son, Joseph, back to Ohio. On a steamboat, Lucy, her mother, Webb, and Ruddy left a few days later.

"…The invasion of Pennsylvania is likely to work important changes; possibly to take us East again. The Army of the Potomac has another commander. I still suspect that in the case of that army, the soldiers are more in fault for their disasters than the generals. I dread to hear of a battle there. They will do better, however, on our own soil. If Grant could only get Vicksburg in time to spare a corps or two of his troops for the campaign in the East, we should be safe enough. If Lee really is pushing into Pennsylvania in full force, it ought to prove his ruin; but we shall see. I think, as you do, that it will do much to unite us.

Sincerely,

R. B. Hayes"

—Hayes to Uncle Sardis

JULY 20, 1863, GALLIPOLIS, OHIO, SAVING THE BUCKEYE STATE

Hayes was a proud Buckeye, long before he signed the order creating The Ohio State University. While in secondary school in Connecticut, he proudly noted the strength of his fellow Buckeyes against those of other classmates, reporting to his mother on July 7, 1838, "P. S. I forgot to tell you that four of us were invited to dinner by one of the boys who lives fifteen miles from here. We walked over there; staid ten hours and walked back by bed time, thirty-six miles in six hours. Three of us were Buckeyes, the other was an Alabamian. Quite pedestrians, the Buckeyes!"

The news of the Union victories at Gettysburg and Vicksburg invigorated the camps all across the North. Hayes, now in charge of the First

Brigade of the Second Division of the Army of Western Virginia, enjoyed the tide turning with his men. On July 16, he found out Confederate Brigadier General John Hunt Morgan had attacked Ohio. Hayes, perhaps thinking back to his plan to save Cincinnati if necessary at the start of the war, asked permission from Scammon to lead a group of his men back home. Scammon was apparently not interested.

Hayes recorded, upon his return on July 22:

"16th [of July], at Fayette—Heard that Morgan was in Ohio at Piketon, leaving there for Gallipolis. General Scammon wisely and promptly determined to head him by sending me. (This was after a sharp controversy.) Seventeenth with Twenty-third and Thirteenth took steamboats from Loup Creek for Gallipolis. 18th at Gallipolis heard Morgan had pushed by up the Ohio as if to cross at Pomeroy.

Sunday, 19th, Pomeroy—Halted; found the militia waiting in position for Morgan. About noon he came; the Twenty-third went out to meet him; found him in force; sent for Thirteenth; formed lines of battle. Morgan ditto. Seeing we were 'regulars and not militia' (words of inspection of Rebels), he hurried off, with some loss. We had one wounded, in his hand—Clemens, Company B.

20th, at daylight—Found Morgan at Buffington Island. He was here attacked by General Judah's cavalry and the gunboats. Not much fighting by Rebels, but great confusion, loss of artillery, etc., etc.

On to Hockingport; guarded the ferries over the Ohio at Lee's Creek, Belleville, and Hocking.

21st, back to Gallipolis—Morgan's army gone up. We got over two hundred prisoners. Everybody got some. No fight in them. The most successful and jolly little campaign we ever had."

Although it was too late to stop Morgan and his men from the raid itself, Hayes defeated the army of 1,200 men and sent a separate message to the Southern military complex. Meade protected Gettysburg, Grant captured Vicksburg, but Hayes put a dot on the exclamation point with his defeat of Morgan and capped off a very successful month of July for the Union cause.

MAY 9, 1864, BLACKSBURG, VIRGINIA, BATTLE AT CLOYD'S MOUNTAIN

The war continued. In the Spring of 1864, under the direction of General George Crook, the Hayes Brigade was tasked with destroying the Virginia and Tennessee Railroad. In the way stood a man named Albert Jenkins, Confederate Brigadier General. He stopped at Cloyd's Mountain to cut off Crook.

The battle was short but intense. Sparks from flint had ignited a leaf bed and men burned alive.[1] Hayes recorded rather stoically:

"May 9—Battle of Cloyd's Mountain, or as Rebs call it 'Cloyd Farm.' Lasted one hour and a half. The Twenty-third and Thirty-sixth, under the immediate direction of General Crook, charged across a meadow three hundred yards wide, sprang into a ditch and up a steep wooded hill to Rebel breastworks, carried them quickly but with a heavy loss. Captain Hunter killed. Lieutenant Seaman ditto. Abbott's left arm shattered. Rice a flesh wound. Eighteen killed outright; about one hundred wounded—many mortally. This in [the] Twenty-third. [The] Thirty-sixth less, as the Twenty-third led the column.

Entered Dublin Depot, ten and one-half miles, about 6:30 P. M. A fine victory. Took some prisoners, about three hundred, five pieces [of] artillery, many stores, etc., etc. A fine country; plenty of forage. My loss, two hundred and fifty [men]."

—*Hayes, diary, May 9, 1864*

In his diary, Hayes is either exhausted or modest. Having pushed the Rebels back in the initial assault, Hayes led a second assault against a familiar foe. Morgan, captured by Hayes at the Run to Gallipolis, had escaped prison and was fortifying Jenkins. Hayes and his men (about 500 including the 23ʳᵈ) broke through again in a very short amount of time.[2]

1. Hoogenboom, *One of the Good Colonels*, 73.
2. Hoogenboom, *One of the Good Colonels*, 73.

MAY 10, 1864, BLACKSBURG, VIRGINIA, IN THE LINE OF FIRE

Following the Battle of Cloyd's Mountain, the Union Army burned the depot of the Virginia and Tennessee Railroad. As they left the next day, Jenkin's army, or what was left of it, protected the New River Bridge. Crook decided to set fire to it as well. Hayes assembled a group of soldiers to serve as a bodyguard for the troops setting the fire. While ordering the men to take cover, one young soldier refused unless Hayes took cover as well. Unfortunately, during the verbal scuffle, the soldier, discovered later to be a woman, was hit with a shell and later died on the riverbank.[1] Crook defeated Jenkins with the Buckeyes leading the way. Hayes and his men were becoming accustomed to such victories. Pedestrian Buckeyes indeed!

That he does not mention it in his diary could mean it did not affect Hayes, but I doubt it. Hayes generally recorded the names of the soldiers he knew personally who have died in battle, or were severely wounded. This young soldier, no matter her gender, was from West Virginia. It is possible Hayes thought it another awful sacrifice of the war.

However, there on the bank of the New River, a young soldier lost her life in an attempt to protect Hayes, or at least convince him to protect himself. Under fire, it was an act of bravery which proves there was a great deal of respect given Hayes by his men and those units surrounding him.

1.   Hoogenboom, *One of the Good Colonels*, 74.

MAY 12, 1864, SALT POND MOUNTAIN, WAGON TRAIN

"Thursday, 12—A most disagreeable rainy day. Mud and roads horrible. Marched from Blacksburg to Salt Pond Mountain. My brigade had charge of the train. I acted as wagon-master; a long train to keep up. Rode all day in mud and rain back and forth. Met "Mudwall" Jackson and fifteen hundred [men]—a poor force that lit out rapidly from near Newport. Got to camp—no tents—[at] midnight. Mud; slept on wet ground without blankets. A horrible day, one of the worst of all my experience. Fifteen miles."

Rutherford Hayes was having a successful, but trying, week. It should be noted, the Civil War was not only fought in the major battles which felled tens of thousands of our soldiers on both sides, but in between in significant smaller ones. The Rebels were willing to fight as long as necessary for what they felt was an attack on their rights. As the war dragged on in 1864 and as the turbulent spring rains allowed, Union armies set out on smaller conquests with no less important results.

The destruction of the railroad was critical to the Union success. It would eventually take six weeks for the South to put the Virginia and Tennessee railroad back in business.[1] Six weeks of time where crucial resources (men, money, and time) were spent repairing rails rather than repelling Yanks. It was a huge victory for Crook and Hayes. But first, they had to get back.

The spring rains were relentless in the Kanawha Valley. Most campaigns did not begin until they were through, but an army must strike while the iron is hot, not to mention somewhat unprotected, and Crook did.

In a personal diary, one with no intent to be read by strangers, we can excuse the writer's attempt at ranking his days. For Hayes, the election of William Henry Harrison was one of the most "glorious" of his life, this one on the wagon train was the "worst." Fifteen miles trudging the caravan through the mud in the pouring rain, only to reach camp in the middle of the night to sleep in the same mud.

Hayes wrote to his uncle:

"Meadow Bluff, Greenbrier County, West Virginia,

May 19, 1864,

Dear Uncle: —We are safely within what we now call 'our own lines' after twenty-one days of marching, fighting, starving, etc., etc. For twelve days we have had nothing to eat except what the country afforded. Our raid has been in all respects successful. We destroyed the famous Dublin Bridge and eighteen miles of the Virginia and Tennessee Railroad and many depots and stores; captured ten pieces of artillery, three hundred prisoners, General Jenkins and other officers among them, and killed and wounded about five hundred, besides utterly routing Jenkins' army in the bloody battle of Cloyd's Mountain.

My brigade had two regiments and part of a third in the battle. [The] Twenty-third lost one hundred killed and wounded. We had a severe duty but did just as well as I could have wished. We charged a Rebel battery entrenched in [on] a wooded hill across an open level meadow three hundred yards wide and a deep ditch, wetting me to the waist, and carried it without a particle of wavering or even check, losing, however, many officers and men killed and wounded. It being the vital point General Crook charged with us in person. One brigade from the Army of the Potomac (Pennsylvania Reserves) broke and fled from the field. Altogether, this is our finest experience in the war, and General Crook is the best general we have ever served under, not excepting Rosecrans.

Many of the men are barefooted, and we shall probably remain here some time to refit. We hauled in wagons to this point, over two hundred of our wounded, crossing two large rivers by fording and ferrying and three ranges of high mountains. The news from the outside world is meagre and from Rebel sources. We almost believe that Grant must have been successful from the little we gather.

Sincerely,

R. B. Hayes"

For Hayes, though proud of the victory, it was indeed a low point. He had no idea what lay ahead but could assume there were more battles, more wounds, and more death around him. What he may have also predicted was continued victory.

He would have been mistaken.

1.　Hoogenboom, *One of the Good Colonels*, 74.

July 24, 1864, Near Winchester, Virginia, Battle of Kernstown

Before the next battle, Hayes learned he was to have a new commanding officer. He was pleased, and wrote to his uncle from Charleston, West Virginia, on July 2, 1864.

"Dear Uncle: —We are told this morning that General Crook is to have the command of the 'Army of the Kanawha,' independent of all control below Grant. If so, good. I don't doubt it. This will secure us the much needed rest we have hoped for and keep us here two or three weeks. My health is excellent, but many men are badly used up.

I do not feel sure yet of the result of Grant's and Sherman's campaigns. One thing I have become satisfied of. The Rebels are now using their last man and last bread. There is absolutely nothing left in reserve. Whip what is now in the field, and the game is ended.

Sincerely,

R. B. Hayes"

Desperation reeked on both sides at the end of July 1864. Grant was pounding Petersburg, Virginia. Crook was looking for Confederate General Jubal Early in Virginia near Winchester.

Hayes in uniform, 1861.

Crook met Early on July 24, 1864. Unfortunately for Crook and his divisions, he did not know it. Suspecting it was just a small band of Rebels, Crook sent Hayes and his men to flush them out.[1]

There would be no flushing. Early attacked Hayes and his men with a barrage of gunfire. Hayes knew immediately the enemy they were facing was more than pickets, skirmishers, or reconnaissance, and he ordered his men to fall back. During the retreat, Hayes was hit on the shoulder, his third wound of the war. Moments later, his horse was shot from under him, sending Hayes tumbling to the ground.[2]

According to author Ari Hoogenboom, "Hayes stand at the stone wall not only enabled Crook's army to escape capture by Early's 17,000-man force but also to withdraw in an orderly fashion."[3]

Hayes wrote to Lucy on July 26 and described the attack, ending with these observations:

"My brigade was in the hottest place and then was in condition to cover the retreat as rear-guard which we did successfully and well for one day and night.

Of course the reason, the place for blame to fall, is always asked in such cases. I think the army is not disposed to blame the result on anybody. The enemy was so superior that a defeat was a matter of course if we fought. The real difficulty was, our cavalry was so inefficient in its efforts to discover the strength of the enemy that General Crook and all the rest of us were deceived until it was too late."

The war, from the Union perspective, was not going well. On July 30, the Rebels burned Chambersburg, Pennsylvania. Fortunately for the North and particularly President Lincoln who was staring a re-election defeat square in the face, General Grant moved quickly. On August 7, Hayes learned General Crook had a new boss, General Philip Sheridan of Ohio. *The Cincinnati Daily Commercial* would write of Sheridan on November 11, 1864, that he is "idolized by the whole army."

Time was running out, and there was much to do. Grant knew Sheridan was just the man to do it.

1. Hoogenboom, *One of the Good Colonels*, 84.

2. Hoogenboom, *One of the Good Colonels*, 84.

3. Hoogenboom, *One of the Good Colonels*, 84.

Rutherford Hayes had a new, enthusiastic general in Philip Sheridan, who pushed his army on the offensive in a relentless drive to finish off the South. Hayes described the action at Berryville to his wife on September 4:

"Dearest: —We had one of the fiercest fights yesterday I was ever in. It was between the South Carolina and Mississippi Divisions under General Kershaw and six regiments of the Kanawha Division. My brigade had the severest fighting, but in loss we none of us suffered as might have been expected. We were under cover except when we charged and then darkness helped. We whipped them, taking about one hundred prisoners and killing and wounding a large number. Captain Gillis was killed, shot near the heart, Captain Austin dangerously wounded through the right shoulder, George Brigdon, my color-bearer, bearing the brigade flag, mortally wounded. Only ten others of [the] Twenty-third hurt. Sixty in the brigade killed or wounded. Captain Gillis was a noble, brave man, a good companion, cheerful and generous—a great loss to us. The Rebel army is again just before us.

It was a pleasant battle to get through, all except the loss of Gillis and Brigdon and Austin. I suppose I was never in so much danger before, but I enjoyed the excitement more than ever before. My men behaved so well. One regiment of another division nearly lost all by running away. The Rebels were sure of victory and run at us with the wildest yells, but our men turned the tide in an instant. This was the crack division of Longstreet. They say they never ran before.

Darling, I think of you always. My apprehension and feeling is a thousand times more for you than for myself. I think we shall have no great battle. We are again entrenched here. Our generals are cautious and wary. —Love to all. The dear boys, God bless them.

Affectionately ever, your R."

Both the diary and letters of Rutherford Hayes, during the period of the Civil War, reveal a man who welcomed the hard road and relished in the fierce fighting. General Crook, just like Colonel Scammon and Rosecrans before him, sent Hayes to the thickest fight, the hottest fire and the most critical junctures because they all knew Hayes could rally his men and get the job done.

Hayes is probably a singular example in the war, describing battles before this as "jolly" and this one as "pleasant" right before admitting he was never in so much danger. Imagine Lucy in Chillicothe, the boys romping at her feet, reading the exploits both proud and scared to death.

Hayes was also an incredibly modest officer. We can imagine no medal or promotion was more important to him than causing Long-street's Rebels to run for the very first time.

SEPTEMBER 19, 1864, OUTSIDE WINCHESTER, VIRGINIA,
BATTLE OF OPEQUON CREEK

Having spent the early years of the Civil War looking for Generals who would move against the South, President Lincoln must have been pleased with his staff as summer ended in 1864. Sheridan pursued Early relentlessly, taking battles every few weeks and sometimes every few days. And Hayes was again, no surprise, thrown into a critical position.

Hayes describes the action to his wife:

"Camp Near Strasburg, Virginia, September 21, 1864,
Dearest: —As I anticipated when I added a few words in pencil to a half finished letter last Sunday, we left camp to seek General Early and give him battle. We met him at Winchester and, as I telegraphed, gained a great victory. General Crook's command in general, and my

brigade and the Second (Kanawha) Division in particular, squared up the balance left against us on the 24th of July at the same place. The fighting began at daylight Monday (19th), with our cavalry. Then the Sixth Corps fighting pretty well, joined in; and about 10:30 A. M. the Nineteenth [Corps] took part—some portions of it behaving badly, losing ground, two guns, and some prisoners. We in the meantime were guarding the wagons (!). Since the fight they say Crook's command was the reserve!

By noon the battle was rather against [us]. The Rebels were jubilant and in Winchester were cheering and rejoicing over the victory. We were sent for. General Crook in person superintended the whole thing. At one o'clock, having passed around on to the Rebel left, we passed under a fire of cannon and musketry and pushed direct for a battery on their extreme flank. This division was our extreme right. My brigade in front, supported by Colonel White's old brigade. As soon as we felt their fire we moved swiftly forward going directly at the battery. The order was to walk fast, keep silent, until within about one hundred yards of the guns, and then with a yell to charge at full speed.

We passed over a ridge and were just ready to begin the rush when we came upon a deep creek with high banks, boggy, and perhaps twenty-five yards wide.

The Rebel fire now broke out furiously. Of course the line stopped. To stop was death. To go on was probably the same; but on we started again. My horse plunged in and mired down hopelessly, just as by frantic struggling he reached about the middle of the stream. I jumped off, and down on all fours, succeeded in reaching the Rebel side—but alone. Perhaps some distance above or below others were across. I was about the middle of the brigade and saw nobody else, but hundreds were struggling in the stream. It is said several were drowned. I think it not true. (N. B. I just received the enclosed with orders to have it read to every man in my division. I send you the original. Save it as precious.) The next man over (I don't know but he beat me—but—) was the adjutant of the Thirty-sixth.

Soon they came flocking, all regiments mixed up—all order gone. [There was] no chance of ever reforming, but pell-mell, over the obstructions, went the crowd. Two cannons were captured; the rest run off. The whole of Crook's Command (both divisions) were soon over, with the general swinging his sword, and the Rebel position was successfully flanked, and victory in prospect for the first time that day.

We chased them three to five hundred yards, when we came in sight of a second line, strongly posted. We steadily worked towards them under a destructive fire. Sometimes we would be brought to a standstill by the storm of grape and musketry, but the flags (yours as advanced as any) would be pushed on and a straggling crowd would follow. With your flag were Twenty-third, Thirty-fourth, Thirty-sixth, and Seventy-first men, and so of all the others. Officers on horseback were falling faster than others, but all were suffering. (Mem.: —Two men got my horse out and I rode him all day, but he was ruined.)

Things began to look dark. The Nineteenth Corps next on our left were in a splendid line, but they didn't push. They stood and fired at long range! Many an anxious glance was cast that way. They were in plain sight, but no, or very little, effective help came from that handsome line. It was too far off. At the most critical moment a large body of that splendid cavalry, with sabres drawn, moved slowly around our right beyond the creek.

Then at a trot and finally with shouts at a gallop [they] charged right into the Rebel lines. We pushed on and away broke the Rebels. The cavalry came back, and an hour later and nearly a mile back, the same scene again; and a third time; and the victory was ours just at sundown.

My division entering Winchester as the Rebels were leaving, far in advance of all other troops. My division commander had fallen (Colonel Duval) badly, not dangerously wounded, and I commanded the division in the closing scenes.

It was a great victory, but a much greater battle to take part in than the results would indicate. I certainly never enjoyed anything more than the last three hours. Dr. Joe was perfectly happy, the last two hours at least—always after the first cavalry charge. We felt well. The sum of it is, [the] Sixth Corps fought well; Nineteenth only so-so. Crook's skill and his men turned the Rebel left making victory possible, and the cavalry saved it when it was in danger of being lost.

Of course this is imperfect. I saw but little of what occurred. For that reason, I would never have a letter of mine shown outside of the family. There is too much risk of errors. For instance, crossing the creek, I could only see one hundred yards or so up and down. Forty men may have beaten me over, but I didn't see them.

Colonel Duval has gone home. I command the division. Colonel Devol of the Thirty-sixth commands the First Brigade in my stead. We are following the retreating Rebels. They will get into an entrenched position before fighting again, and I suspect we shall not assault them in strong works. So I look for no more fighting with General Early this campaign. —Love to all.

Affectionately, R."

Earlier in the year on May 12, Hayes had experienced what he called then the worst day in his life, trudging through deep mud on a trail with a wagon train. But he made it through. Perhaps he thought of that day as he stood in front of 100 yards of sure treachery, deep mud, but this time under intense fire.

There are two amazing moments in Hayes life during this short period of one single day. First, when he charged into the mud facing certain death to begin, and second, the moment he dismounted his horse and finished the obstacle on his hands and knees. The man was resilient. The man was tough. And mercifully, the man was not done.

SEPTEMBER 22, 1864, NEAR STRASBURG, VIRGINIA,
BATTLE OF FISHER'S HILL

Sheridan pressed on towards the fleeing Early, determined to finish him off. Sheridan had two options in the next round on September 22. He favored a frontal assault, but Crook and Hayes, who by his rank and friendship with Crook also attended the war council, favored an assault on the left flank up Little North Mountain. Someone in the room suggested the climb was impossible, advising, "Nothing but a crow could go up there."[1]

Nothing but a crow, and Rutherford B. Hayes. Hayes convinced Crook and Crook convinced Sheridan. The battle was met, the surprise worked, the men yelled and ran, and the Rebels fled.

The battles were short, but the rewards in captured Rebels and weaponry were immense. Even more so, the Union Army running over Rebels seemingly at will, in the Old Dominion, was demoralizing to the public and to the government trying to hold the Rebellion together.

But perhaps, as a possum cornered in the barn, there was one good strike left in the Southern Cause.

1. Hoogenboom, *One of the Good Colonels*, 94.

OCTOBER 11, 1864, CHILLICOTHE, OHIO, BIRTH OF SON GEORGE CROOK

The words "jolly" and "pleasant" dropped from the letters Hayes wrote home as 1864 began to wane. According to Hoogenboom, for the first time Hayes was beginning to grow tired of the war.[1]

He had just turned forty-two years old, the fourth birthday away from home in as many years. He hoped to be home at Christmas to see his new son, named for his friend and favorite general, George Crook.

But there was one more battle to be fought before 1864 would end. And unfortunately on the Union side, no one saw it coming.

1. Hoogenboom, *One of the Good Colonels*, 95.

OCTOBER 19, 1864, NEAR MIDDLETOWN, VIRGINIA, BATTLE OF CEDAR CREEK

The possum struck back one last time at Cedar Creek, catching everyone off guard, including Sheridan who had journeyed to Washington for briefings. In the confusion and retreat of the beginning stages of the battle, Hayes lost his horse from under him and fell to the ground with such a force those that witnessed the accident thought he had been killed. But he got up.

Confusion reigned until Sheridan returned from Washington and rallied the exhausted troops to victory. But the story is better told by Hayes himself:

"Camp at Cedar Creek near Strasburg, Virginia,
October 21, 1864,

My Darling: —We have had another important victory over General Early's oft-defeated army. Reinforced by a division or two of Longstreet's Corps, he was foolish enough to follow and attack us here on the 19th. In the darkness and fog of early morning he was successful in doubling up our left flank, held by General Crook's little First Division, and so flanking our whole army out of its position, capturing for the time our camps, a good many cannon, and perhaps fifteen hundred prisoners. But soon after it got light, we began to recover and finally checked and held them.

In the afternoon we took the offensive and without much difficulty or loss flogged them completely, capturing all their cannon, trains, etc., etc., and retaking all we had lost besides many prisoners. The Rebels marched off a part of our prisoners. For a time things looked squally, but the truth is, all the fighting capacity of Early's army was taken out of it in the great battle at Winchester a month ago. My loss was small. In the Thirteenth Lieutenant-Colonel Hall, a conspicuously brave and excellent officer, was killed. Lieutenant McBride (of [the] Twelfth) was wounded in [the] Twenty-third; two officers of [the] Fifth [Virginia] ditto.

As usual with me I had some narrow escapes. While galloping rapidly, my fine large black horse was killed instantly, tumbling heels over head and dashing me on the ground violently. Strange to say I was only a little bruised and was able to keep the saddle all day...I was also hit fairly in the head by a ball which had lost its force in getting (I suppose) through somebody else! It gave me only a slight shock—I think serious fighting on this line is now over.

I suppose you are pleased with the result of the election. Of course, I am, on general reasons. My particular gratification is much less than it would be, if I were not so much gratified by my good luck in winning "golden opinions" in the more stirring scenes around me here. My share of notoriety here is nothing at all, and my real share of merit is also small enough, I know, but the consciousness that I am doing my part in these brilliant actions is far more gratifying than anything the election brings me.

Love to all. I am more than anxious to see you again.

Affectionately ever, your R."

Perhaps the best proof of the homesickness and utter exhaustion felt by Hayes is the brief mention of his promotion in his diary:

"Tuesday, 3—Bright day. Walked up Wills Creek to the Narrows. Received appointment as brigadier-general, dated November 30, to rank from October 19, 'for gallantry and meritorious services in the battles of Opequon, Fisher's Hill, and Middletown.' Put on shoulder-straps worn by General Crook in Tennessee. Changed quarters from Revere House to St. Nicholas."

He was even succinct with his wife in a letter dated January 5, 1865:

"The publication of my appointment has been made. I have not yet got the original document. It was mis-sent to New York City and will go from there to Chillicothe. If it gets there before I do you will open it. It gives as the reason of the appointment, gallantry and good conduct in the late battles in the Shenandoah Valley and dates from the Battle of Cedar Creek, October 19, 1864.

Aside from the vanity which goes always with brass buttons, I have other reasons for wanting the grounds of the appointment published. No flourish of trumpets, no comment, but simply, 'Colonel R. B. Hayes, Twenty-third Regiment O. V. I., has been appointed brigadier-general' for (here quote the exact words of the appointment)."

The "other reasons" Hayes had in mind for the publication was probably due the fact he was nominated and elected to Congress from Cincinnati without stepping foot back in Ohio the entire length of the election.

JANUARY 21, 1865, CAMP HASTINGS, KIDNAPPED?

The boyhood hero-worship of George Washington may have saved Hayes' life in early 1865, as the officer corps, including General Crook, was kidnapped in a desperation effort by the Rebels on January 21. From his diary:

"Shriver Mansion, January 21—At 3:30 A. M. Captain McNeal and fifty or so of his band kidnapped Generals Kelley and Crook from their hotel on Baltimore Street. Daring and well executed. They inquired for me but on learning that I quartered in camp did not look further."

In a letter to Lucy dated January 23, 1864, Hayes ends with this revealing postscript:

"P. S. —The Rebels inquired for me, but were informed that I quartered with my troops. If it could be without stain I would rather like now to be captured. It would be a good experience."

Apparently, the rest Hayes needed was fulfilling its course, he was back to his old self again, relishing the life of a Civil War officer and wishing, even at this point unbelievably so, he would have been captured—just for the experience. Did Ian Fleming actually base his fearless James Bond character on this man Rutherford Hayes?

The war was finally coming to a close. Hayes writes on January 22:

"Sherman took Columbia Friday, the 18th. Rebels evacuated Charleston Tuesday, 15th. Today at noon national salute here and everywhere because 'the old flag floats again over Sumter.'"

APRIL 16, 1865, NEW CREEK, WEST VIRGINIA

"Dear Uncle: —I am in receipt of yours of the 11th. My mountain expedition is given up. If I go at all from here, it will be directly up the valleys to occupy Staunton. In any event, I think I shall see no more active campaigning.

I have been greatly shocked by the tragedy at Washington. At first it was wholly dark. So unmerited a fate for Lincoln! Such a loss for the country! Such a change! But gradually, consolatory topics suggest themselves. How fortunate that it occurred no sooner!

Now the march of events will neither be stopped nor changed. The power of the Nation is in our armies, and they are commanded by such men as Grant, Sherman, and Thomas, instead of McClellan, Hooker, or, etc., etc. Lincoln's fame is safe. He is the Darling of History evermore. His life and achievements give him titles to regard second to those of no other man in ancient or modern times. To these, this tragedy now adds the crown of martyrdom.

Sincerely, R."

JUNE 8, 1865, WASHINGTON, DC, COMMISSION RESIGNED

Four years and five days following his initial decision to enter the war, Rutherford Hayes was leaving it. After all, he had work to do, and a duty to fulfill in the United States Congress. As he left the army, he was honored with the rank of Major General for his conduct in 1864.

"Dear Mother: We are once more all together in good health. The three larger boys are all going to school and are improving in their books. Little George is a very fine-looking and promising child.

We had a pleasant trip to Richmond…I expect to go to Cincinnati in a few days and will probably be at Delaware to spend Sunday with you. I am now out of the army. Laura and General Mitchell will come home soon. General Mitchell has also resigned and will be out of the army in a few days.

I am very happy to be through with the war.

Affectionately, your son,

Rutherford, Chillicothe, June 11, 1865."

Happy indeed. Rutherford Hayes, the volunteer officer, had mastered war like a seasoned West Point general. Fighting alongside his men under the most insane circumstances, under heavy fire with men falling around him, Hayes deserves the most glowing praise which he himself would have shrugged off. His "duty" compelled him to serve. And he was a brilliant, courageous, mighty warrior.

Future President McKinley, who served the entire war under Hayes, had this to say of the man he considered a father figure: "His whole nature seemed to change when in battle. From the sunny, agreeable, the kind, the generous, the gentle gentleman…he was, once the battle was on, intense and ferocious."

Happy he was. Five times wounded, four horses shot from under him, Rutherford Hayes was ready to go home. He would seamlessly turn from service to his country on the battle field to service in the halls of Congress.

Politics...

"My Darling: I reached the depot here about six P. M. yesterday, the boys with Rock met me and had me up to the house in a 'jiffy,' as Mother used to say. Both the boys laughing and talking—as tanned as Indians and jolly as porpoises. Birch chops and hauls dirt for the road and Webb rows boat and fishes on the river. School of course but secondary. Their talk was of chickens.

The flower garden has more plants in it, and will someday amount to something. Your verbenas (is that right?) will go into a star-shaped bed tomorrow. The rains have brought up the grass everywhere. It is a beautiful place.

Birch calls me 'Dad' with great complacency and lays his hand on my shoulder familiarly. Have had a pleasant day with the boys. Very happy little (or big) fellows they are, and very happy it is to be with them. —Good night. Love to all.
Sincerely, your
    R."

— *Hayes to Lucy, Fremont, June 2, 1867*

OCTOBER 12, 1864, CINCINNATI, OHIO, ELECTION TO CONGRESS

"An officer fit for duty who at this crisis would abandon his post to electioneer for a seat in Congress ought to be scalped. You may feel perfectly sure I shall do no such thing."

—*Hayes to William Henry Smith, August 24, 1864*

Rutherford Hayes did not cultivate a habit of promoting himself. His lifelong sense of 'duty' propelled him to the forefront of his day. His personal policy was to do what was right and the promotions would come. That guidepost served him in the first political office since he was defeated in his re-election for City Solicitor of Cincinnati a month before he entered the war.

He was nominated to serve as a United States congressman by his peers in Cincinnati in August of 1864. When asked to come home to campaign, Hayes responded to his good friend and newspaperman, William Smith, with the above statement, a quip sure to catch fire in the city.

Instead, newspapers in Cincinnati, along with daily casualty reports, were carrying advertisements of the "Union Ticket" and listing Gen. Rutherford B. Hayes on the ballot for the Second Congressional District.

Already familiar in Cincinnati, his honorable service in the war notwithstanding, he won the election by 2,400 votes, not having stepped foot in the district during the entire cavass. He was elated, but Congress would not convene until December of 1865.

In the meantime, the intense heat of the battlefield was replaced by the intense pressure from office-seekers. They were as relentless as Jubal Early himself.

May 24, 1866, Cincinnati, Ohio, Son George Crook Dies

Sophia Hayes had worried constantly over her son, "Rud," the first two years of his life. As it was in the early 1820s, so too in the middle of the 1860s. The Hayes' fourth son became the second child to die within the first two years of his life on May 24, 1866. It would be the first of two emotional losses for Hayes in the time span of six months. George Crook gone in the dawn of his life, Mother Sophia would follow in the twilight of hers.

October 30, 1866, Columbus, Ohio, Mother Sophia Dies

"Dear Guy: —I would have sent the enclosed letter as to Stephen's affair before, but I have been absent attending in the last sickness and at the funeral of my mother at Columbus and Delaware. She died without pain in the possession of her faculties to the last, and confident of the future. She was almost seventy-five years of age. Uncle Birchard was with her and the most of her grandchildren.

My regards to your wife and little folks.

As ever,

R. B. Hayes, Cincinnati, November 5, 1866"

"**M**en are what their Mothers made them," said Ralph Waldo Emerson. Hayes loved Emerson, and the epitaph fits the special bond between Rutherford and his mother Sophia. Born six months following the death of his own father, Sophia and Rutherford shared a bond which leaps from the pages of his diary and their letters.

Both doting and stubborn, the exchanges, as mentioned earlier in this text, beautifully crest from Mother shepherding son, to son teasing Mother.

"Mother wants me to like my teachers. Well, I do like them—a great ways off. She says I must not think my teachers are partial. Well, I don't think they are. I know so; and do believe they are partial to me—for one. Mother told me to begin a letter on receipt of hers. I did so, and then burnt it. She says I must be careful of my health. Well, I is careful. She also says I must dry my clean clothes by the fire. Well, if I did that I should put none on."

—Rutherford to Fanny, February 5, 1839

To his Mother, he was sickeningly stubborn at age seventeen:

"…what pleased me particularly was your saying I must 'bring my clothes home,' as if I would forget to wear any. You say I missed seeing many friends by not being home, but if I had not been here I should not have seen some of my friends…"

—Rutherford to Sophia, March 10, 1839

She was laid to rest next to her husband, Rutherford Sr., in Delaware, Ohio. For all the glory and honor this book has heaped on the man Hayes, may it be suggested the same heralds are laid at the feet of his mother, Sophia, who made him.

Deep in a campaign swing across his beloved Buckeye State, Hayes made haste to Cincinnati for the birth of the couple's fifth child, a daughter. The same man who saved a random woman on the day he proposed marriage was the same man who was not about to miss the child's birth. Lucy's biographer, Emily Apt Geer, relates the following morsel, "According to a family story," due to uncooperative train schedules, "he commandeered a railroad handcar for the last thirty-eight miles of the journey."[1]

Consider the myriad of tales told in song and film in modern times on this very subject—a father frantically risking life and limb to be back in time for a child's birth. Hayes needs his own song.

Lucy's husband made it on time. And there was only one name considered for their new child, a daughter: Fanny. She would become, much like the sister for whom she was named, the light of Rutherford Hayes' life.

1. Geer, Emily Apt, *First Lady, The Life of Lucy Webb Hayes*, (Kent State University Press, 1984), 94.

"My Dear Uncle: —You need not be told how much the result of the election disappoints me. You know I will bear it cheerfully and with philosophy. It is however a puzzling thing to decide now what is next to be done. Assuming that I am beaten, which I do not doubt, I must choose my path anew. I will see you and talk it all over soon. No man in my place would probably have done differently, but the thing is over, and now for a sensible future. I feel sorry for the boys—especially Birch.

I hope your health is good, and that you will borrow no trouble on account of this.

Sincerely,

R. B. Hayes, Cincinnati, October 9, 1867"

The name Hayes began floating around for governor as early as 1864. Local Republican leaders in the 1860's were as lazy and uncreative then as they are now. They did not see the merit in the distinguished service of Hayes and other Civil War heroes, but a last name easily recognizable due to the incessant coverage of the newspapers.

To be sure, Hayes was very interested in being governor, but he would run when he was ready. Nominated in June 1867, he set upon the campaign on August 5, sometimes speaking twice-a-day across the state.[1] On October 8, Ohio went to the polls to vote for a governor, a senator, their representatives and the 15th Amendment to the Constitution, guaranteeing African American's the right to vote.

With a total vote of 484,000, every Republican was defeated as well as the proposed Constitutional Amendment. As Hayes noted above, he thought he had lost, too. Election tallies in 1867 were still slow, and the rumors ran as rampant as the ones declaring the locations of Confederate generals just five years previous. This would not be his first defeat, so Hayes was prepared.

But the outcome was certain a few days later. He had defeated Democrat Allen Thurman by almost 2,500 votes.[2]

And he would make equal rights his badge of honor.

1. Hoogenboom, *Rutherford B. Hayes, Warrior and President*, 211.
2. Hoogenboom, *Rutherford B. Hayes, Warrior and President*, 214.

JANUARY 13, 1868, COLUMBUS, OHIO,

FIRST INAUGURAL ADDRESS, GOVERNOR

Hayes worked hard on his inaugural address, and was proud of its short length. He sent an advance copy to his uncle with this letter:

"Dear Uncle: —I suppose you are entitled to an advance copy of my inaugural. Here it is. It contains but three [ideas]. First, a compliment to Governor Cox; second, advice against too much legislation; and third, it shows that I still stand by equal suffrage. It is the shortest ever delivered in Ohio.

Our new home is most agreeable. I can give you a pleasant room with an air-tight wood-stove and a bedroom opening into it, so much like your own that I am sure you would be safe in health and feel at home.

Sincerely,

R. B. Hayes, Columbus, Ohio, January 11, 1868"

Rutherford Hayes in 1868.

Rutherford Hayes was sworn in as the twenty-ninth governor of Ohio on January 13, 1868. The same day as the inauguration, he sent off another letter to his uncle, including a new copy of his speech. Because, "I found our Democrats foolish enough to be repealing Ohio's assent to the Fourteenth Amendment. So I put in some words on that head. —All well."

Hayes would come to enjoy being governor. He would be free to put time into the pursuits he believed in, pursuits which would make him a valuable member of modern society just as he was in 1867. And each of these causes stemmed from his personal life. Prison reform, equal rights, pensions for wounded veterans, improved care for the sick and invalid, and education.

He was also the chief supporter behind the memorial to Abraham Lincoln at the Ohio Capitol which includes the beautiful carving of Grant at Vicksburg.

In a letter to his uncle, Hayes pointed out another program for which he was excited:

"Columbus, April 3, 1869,

Dear Uncle: —The best thing of my administration, I suspect, will be the beginning of the geological survey. It carried very handsomely in both branches. Now comes the important point. Who is to be chief geologist? My prepossessions are for Professor Newberry. Please ask Mr. Bushnell about it and get him to write me, showing him or telling him what I say.

Sincerely,

R. B. Hayes"

Add scientist to the list of adjectives to describe Hayes, albeit from the standpoint of promoting science. The survey would place emphasis on Ohio's vast natural reserves, but was forward-thinking and crucial to the future development of the state.

October 12, 1869, Columbus, Ohio, Re-elected Governor

During his first term as governor, Hayes faced a Democratic legislature and was without the ability to veto legislation. One of the sole 'gifts' the Democratic representatives presented to Hayes was the funding for the geological survey. Perhaps the second term would be politically brighter.

It was. Almost as if he was back in the Kanawha Valley with the 23rd, Hayes' opponent, George Pendleton, was as easy to tail as Jubal Early. Though Hayes, as was his custom, prepared himself for defeat the night of election day, he was resoundingly re-elected with a Republican majority. His plurality for governor was three times that of 1867.

War hero, two-term governor, all before the age of fifty. It would not be long before party leaders would begin pushing Hayes to run for president.

JANUARY 3, 1870, COLUMBUS, OHIO, THE ANNUAL
MESSAGE AND THE SEEDS OF OHIO STATE

Rutherford Hayes had been governor for two years and was beginning to hit his stride. His annual message, delivered in December, continued to focus on those who Hubert Humphrey would have said were in the "shadows of society," as well as an act to finance a new university which the Ohio Legislature had been ignoring.

"I now begin to collect materials and set down a few items for my annual message: —

1. Fifteenth Amendment—a few words of emphatic recommendation and approval.
2. Soldiers' Orphans' Homes.
3. Reform, improvement, or progress in prison discipline.
4. The Re-appraisement.
5. The Geological Survey.

Portrait of then Governor Hayes, 1868.

6. Inebriate Asylum.

7. Incurable Insane.

8. Agricultural fund; college to be located,

... Take up the benevolent and reformatory institutions; give their condition, number of inmates, cost, etc., etc. (See Governor Chase's message 1860.)

... To recommend clearly and briefly the things deemed best without argument or illustration." (December 2, 1869)

Item number eight just happens to be the pre-cursor to what would become The Ohio State University. The legislature, up to this point, had not acted on the Morrill Land Grant Act signed by President Lincoln in 1862.

And then this:

"Columbus, December 7, 1869,

Dear Sir: —I concur with your views of prison discipline so far as I know them. In my next message I wish to say a few words recommending the creation of a prison for young offenders to be conducted on the principles of your report of December, 1868, (Twenty-fourth Annual Report), and to call attention in a general way to the Irish convict system. The present Board of Directors and the Warden of the Ohio Penitentiary are prepared to take enlightened and humane action.

But I do not anticipate the immediate adoption of your theory. My desire is to say enough to open the subject to the consideration of the people of the State. If you have issued, or can refer me to any new publications on the subject, I will be glad to send you their cost.

Sincerely,

R. B. Hayes.

E. C. Wines,

Prison Association of New York"

In our modern era, politicians, even private citizens have only one major cause upon which they tether their ball. Hayes, on the other hand, took on every reform, for every age, every class and seemed to reach out to every "less fortunate" person. The James Bond of the Civil War had morphed into a cross between Bob Hope and Martin Luther King, Jr. as governor. And he relished the opportunities.

JANUARY 27, 1870, COLUMBUS, OHIO, 15TH AMENDMENT PASSES OHIO

Rutherford Hayes was not an abolitionist. But he was an ardent supporter of equal rights. He fought four long years and endured every known hardship short of amputation in the Civil War. He fought for the emancipation of African Americans and made no attempt to temper his opinion they deserved the right to vote. He campaigned on it, and he intended to govern on it.

The vote to ratify the 15th Amendment was defeated once in 1869 by the Democrats. On January 27, 1870, it was brought to a vote for a second time. The language is this:

"Section 1. The right of citizens of the United States to vote shall not be denied or abridged by the United States or by any State on account of race, color, or previous condition of servitude.

Section 2. The Congress shall have power to enforce this article by appropriate legislation."[1]

The vote was razor thin. Fifty-seven to fifty-five in the Assembly and nineteen to eighteen in the Senate.[2] Ohio was one of the final states to vote for ratification.

1. *The United States Constitution*, National Archives.

2. Hoogenboom, *Rutherford B. Hayes, Warrior and President*, 226.

MARCH 30, 1870, COLUMBUS, OHIO,
15TH AMENDMENT BECOMES NATIONAL LAW

Rutherford Hayes would admit, as the Republicans came calling on him in 1876 to run for president, that with the ratification of the 15th Amendment, there was little left to do. He felt his work was complete, his battle wounds justified, and the country moving forward with the inclusion of this basic equal right extended to all male citizens. (Women would not receive the right to vote until 1920.)

March 30 was a special day in his life, as the bullets fired in war were replaced by votes cast in the ballot box.

APRIL 4, 1870, CINCINNATI, OHIO,
WITNESS TO FIRST AFRICAN AMERICANS VOTING

"April 4, 1870—Went to Cincinnati to the election. The colored people vote for the first time under the Fifteenth Amendment. They are very happy and the people generally approve. They vote Republican almost solid."

In the same city which voted him out in an anti-Republican rage in 1861, he witnessed a peaceful transition as African Americans lined up to vote. That he traveled there as governor to watch the proceedings take place reveals (again!) what kind of man he was. Even in modern times, such a trip would be shut down as suicide, political or otherwise. But Hayes thrilled in being at the center of the action. If he was not in Cincinnati on the first election after ratification, he might as well have been on the dark side of the moon.

JANUARY 19, 1871, OHIO STATE CAPITOL BUILDING,
DEDICATION OF MEMORIAL TO LINCOLN AND THE OHIO SOLDIERS

Each day at the Ohio State Capitol, schoolchildren, dignitaries, and citizens of Ohio gaze upon the bust of President Abraham Lincoln and the beautiful relief of Grant's victory at Vicksburg. What the visitors may not realize is the Memorial was the pet project of citizen and then Governor Rutherford Hayes.

This is a lasting memorial that everyone should know is due to Hayes. The night of the dedication, Hayes the politician does something altogether unusual. Reacting to the dignity of the moment, he decides not to give a speech he had prepared. Name one national politician today who would choose to be silent rather than speak?

"I did an unusual, and, I think, a meritorious, thing last night. Tom Jones' Memorial to Lincoln and the Ohio Soldiers was to be inaugurated in the rotunda of the Capitol. I presided. I had a fairish little opening speech, which with my good lungs I could make go off well. But there were three speakers to give addresses. I knew that the little, pretty, pet things to be said were not numerous, and that my speech would more or less interfere with the success of theirs. I accordingly swallowed my speech and introduced the various actors without an extra word. Who has beaten this?

The speech I didn't make:

Fellow Citizens: —We have assembled this evening to witness the inauguration, the unveiling of a Memorial—the work of an Ohio sculptor, Thomas D. Jones, of Cincinnati—placed here in the rotunda of the State House, to remain, we trust, as long as the building itself shall stand, in honor of the brave sons of Ohio who in more than a thousand conflicts on land and water poured out their lives for Liberty and Union; and in honor also of him who 'strove for the right as God gave him to see the right,' and who 'with charity for all and malice towards none,'

'Ascended Fame's ladder so high, From the round at the top he stepped in the sky.'"

—Hayes, diary, January 20, 1871

OCTOBER 10, 1871, CHICAGO, ILLINOIS, AFTER THE FIRE

On October 8, 1871, the city of Chicago experienced a fire of epic proportions, eventually destroying 2,000 acres of the city. In Ohio, Rutherford Hayes was voting for the last time as governor. He had decided against a third term and looked forward to moving to Fremont and establishing himself at the home of his uncle at Spiegel Grove.

But first, he went to Chicago:

"October 10—After voting went with Force to Chicago to see the big fire and help the sufferers.

October 11—General Sheridan gave me fine quarters at his house. Sent me with his ambulance to visit the ruins."

While he and his son Force toured the area, he ran into his old friend William Henry Smith, who recalled,

"I accidentally met Governor Hayes as he was slowly walking over the debris and contemplating the extent and thoroughness of the destruction. It must have been in the vicinity of Madison and Wells Streets (Fifth Avenue). There was not a single wall in that vicinity left above the general level-not one brick upon another.

In the gloomy state of mind I then was, the sight of an old friend was the next best thing to the restoration of the city. His cheerful face and manner and earnest words of encouragement acted like magic, and I soon found myself taking a hopeful view of the future. We proceeded across the river to the office on Canal Street from which Mr. Medill had been issuing his Tribune since the 10th, and after a few moments' conversation with that gentleman, the governor wrote a brief address to the citizens of Ohio, which I caused to be sent in the Associated Press report."

—William Henry Smith, RBH online diary collection

In his address to the people of Ohio, Hayes encouraged them to send money, for which he made the first deposit of $100 to help the people of Chicago.[1]

1. Hoogenboom, *Rutherford B. Hayes, Warrior and President*, 235.

JANUARY 9, 1872, COLUMBUS, OHIO, STILL ABOUT DUTY

On his last day as governor, Hayes recorded his accomplishments.

"Acts I have urged the Legislature to adopt or otherwise contributed to:
  1. Geological Survey.
  2. Soldiers' Orphans' Home.

3. Board of State Charities.

4. Removal of Central Lunatic Asylum out of the city of Columbus.

5. Provision for the chronic insane.

6. A graded prison, enlargement of prison, improvement of prison discipline.

7. Minority representation.

8. Agricultural college.

9. Governor's portraits.

10. The suffrage amendment to the Constitution of Ohio, 1867.

11. The Fifteenth Amendment to the Constitution of the United States, 1869.

12. The Lincoln Memorial —T. D. Jones.

13. Inebriate Asylum.

14. Right to vote of disabled volunteers at National Asylum at Dayton.

15. Right to vote of visible admixtures.

16. Right to vote of college students.

17. Collection of pioneer sketches, letters, and other manuscripts, throwing light on pioneer history; purchase of St. Clair papers.

18. Collection of work of the mound-builders.

19. Took ground that no more public debts ought to be allowed.

20. As to judges—mode of appointing-term of office, salaries.

21. Girls' Reformatory.

22. Monuments to Generals Harrison and Hamer.

I have appointed political adversaries on important boards, viz., Agricultural College, Soldiers' Orphans' Home, the Commission on Mining and Strikes. At first the attempt to put a Democrat on each board was resisted in the Senate of the State. I was assailed as untrue to my party, but the advantages of minority representation were soon apparent, and the experiment became successful."

—Hayes, diary, January 9, 1872

Hayes was proud of his record, but also longed to retire and looked forward to uniting his young family at a new home in Fremont.

Party leadership had other plans. Allow Hayes to begin the tale:

"Last night, after I had put out the lights and was about retiring, the bell was rung. On coming down and opening the door, a senator, General Casement, and Ford, a representative, both Republicans, entered. I took them into the parlor. The senator began promptly:

'Well, I come to business at once. We want to make you Senator. There are eight Republicans, three senators and five representatives, who are ready to stand in the breach. John Sherman is a corrupt man and ought to be defeated. I have nothing personal against him. He and his brothers have always treated me well, but he is utterly corrupt, and I mean to beat him. We can do it, if you will consent. There are many Republicans who are opposed to him, but they will vote for him on one or two ballots, yielding to the majority. His defeat is certain if you consent. Besides, the man now elected senator over the caucus will be the next president of the United States.'

This is the substance of his talk. It was earnest and rapid, at times somewhat warm. The representative was less confident, but felt sure of five or six who would bolt to elect either Hayes or Garfield. Names were given and other particulars. My reply was that, with my views of duty, I could not honorably consent and would not.

The senator said it was strange to see the senatorship refused with the Presidency in prospect. The conversation lasted perhaps fifteen minutes. I made the point on them that they were now committed to Sherman themselves; that the public would so regard it; that their votes in caucus and in the Legislature were totally inconsistent with their present efforts...

I urged the importance of not splitting the Republican party; of electing a Republican president once more, at least; that the defeat of Grant now was to give the Government to the enemies of the recent amendments

Hayes circa 1870.

and to unsettle all. The senator said he was not hostile to Grant, but Grant had done many bad things and his defeat by a good Republican would be a good thing. At last he asked: 'Well, if we vote for and elect you, will you not accept?'

I replied that my decision applied to the whole thing; that I would not be used for the purpose he wished in any way, or under any circumstances. They left with handshakings and the remark by the senator that it was 'strange to see a man throw away the senatorship.'

I went to bed after telling it to Lucy who laughed and said she would not sleep now for fear of some Democrat slipping in."

Amazingly, Hayes repeated the story again with different characters after he had put on his nightshirt. At the end of the second conversation, Hayes stood firm:

"This was all said rapidly with no pause to hear from me. I said: 'Well, I can't honorably do it and there is no use talking; it is settled and has been for weeks.' He said: 'Well, if you say that, I must give it up. I admire your principle, but John Sherman wouldn't do it. Say nothing about this.' And he returned to his carriage and I to sleep. The senator [had] said at parting, 'This ought to be private, but it is among gentlemen and I need say nothing.'

The election by joint convention of the two houses will take place today at noon. I am curious to see what these gentlemen will do. Lucy says: 'Thank fortune we don't want to be elected that way…'"

Twice in the middle of the night, Hayes was offered a seat in the United States Senate. Lesser men with lesser minds would have snatched it right out of their hands, and out of the hands of John Sherman, brother of General William Tecumseh Sherman.

This is included in the days which stand out in the life of Hayes because it showcases his great honor, even for people he did not necessarily know, in this case John Sherman. In the coming years, John Sherman would enter the Hayes administration and become a critical member of the circle during the tumultuous days of the Hayes White House. Hayes may not have seen it this way, but he had just been barely hit with a bullet slowed by going through someone else.

OCTOBER 4, 1872, CINCINNATI, BROCK'S HALL, DEFEATED FOR CONGRESS

"Today I am fifty years old. My darling came down with our dear little Fanny last night and both are now in the room—Lucy lying on the lounge and little Fanny busy washing the articles on the washstand. A happy family. My last speech of the campaign will be made today, tonight rather, at Cumminsville. I prefer to be elected, but am not at all solicitous about it. I don't want to go to Washington. The chances are about even, as I see them today. It has been a pleasant canvass. Some treachery in our camp. But good people encourage me."

—Hayes, diary, October 4, 1872

Fortunately, Hayes lost the election to Congress in a landslide for presidential candidate Horace Greeley, one of the lone landslides Greeley would enjoy as he was soundly defeated by Grant across the rest of the nation. But Hayes went down.

He wrote to his uncle:

"Cincinnati, October 9, 1872,

Dear Uncle: —You will know of our Waterloo defeat in Cincinnati long before this reaches you. It is complete and overwhelming; so complete that it leaves no personal sting. In fact, my share in it is rather pleasant. I am largely ahead of my ticket.

At the close of the polls my election was conceded at the Enquirer office. I met no one who doubted it. I seemed to be the only man who appreciated the load. And I was surprised at its size. The slips I enclose show how well it leaves my record. I have no regrets. The result of the presidential business is most happy. We can rejoice over that.

We will not come up until next week sometime. Health good.

Sincerely,

R. B. Hayes"

MAY 3, 1873, FREMONT, OHIO, SETTLED AT SPIEGEL GROVE

Sardis Birchard purchased the land, which would eventually become Spiegel Grove, in 1846. All his life, Rutherford was a constant visitor to the property, as well as to the uncle who had served as a father his entire life, without fail. With the exception of cousins and distant relatives in New England, Uncle Sardis was the last link of the Hayes family chain which led him to his mother Sophia and sister Fanny.

It was always intended that Hayes and his family should settle with Sardis at Spiegel Grove, named such because the large trees created pools which reflected light like a mirror. "Spiegel" means "mirror" in German.

Finally, following the defeat for Congress, Hayes was coming 'home.' He recorded in his diary the start of a new life with a new resolution:

"May 2. Friday—Today Uncle rode out for the first time since December 11. Dr. Stilwell took charge of him. He was very anxious to get out into the open air. He feels that there is danger of becoming deranged and dreads it very much. He is quite nervous at times. I have a dispatch from Uncle Joe telling me to meet Lucy at Lima Saturday, the third. Then we will all be at Fremont, except the two older at Cornell.

Our return, or rather my return, and our settlement at Fremont will date from May 3, 1873. I left Fremont for Cincinnati in 1849 and now come back, having achieved as much as I expected, or even hoped, by my life in Cincinnati, with kindly feelings towards all the world, to spend the closing years in the home of my youth, and the favorite resort of my childhood.

Let me resolve to lead a good and useful life, characterized by kindness, friendliness, and liberality; taking more care of my children and their training and culture than ever before, and loving my darling wife, and contributing more than ever to her comfort and happiness."

AUGUST 1, 1873, SPIEGEL GROVE, FREMONT, OHIO,
BIRTH OF SON, MANNING FORCE

The sixth son of Rutherford and Lucy Hayes was born on August 1, 1873, at Spiegel Grove. Lucy was just short of forty-two years old and the birth was frightful. According to Lucy Hayes' biographer Emily Apt Geer, son Webb Hayes, overhearing his mother's torment in the house, was taken aback when told he had a new brother, believing she was sick, potentially with cholera.[1]

The son was named for the governor's friend, General Manning Force, commander of the 20th Ohio Volunteer Infantry who was disfigured in the Battle of Atlanta in 1864.

1. Geer, *First Lady, The Life of Lucy Webb Hayes*, 106–107.

"Uncle is fond of repeating the reply made by someone to the question, 'My friend, why do you talk so much to yourself?' 'Well,' replied the questionee, 'I will tell you. I talk to myself because I like to talk to a sensible man, and because I like to hear a sensible man talk.'"

Uncle Sardis had always planned that Rutherford and his family would join him in retirement. He would tragically only enjoy their company for one year. Hayes adored his uncle, and it shows in his reflection on the day of his death:

"January 29, 1874—The twenty-first of January, 1874, was a dismal day. The fog in Fremont was the heaviest ever known. Uncle had passed a comfortable night and was able to get up as usual and go around the house. He shaved himself and was quite comfortable until about eleven o'clock A. M. He had lain down after looking at the work going on finishing the new house belonging to Miss Grant [where he had been living for some time]. Mrs. Grant sang to him 'When I can read my title clear.'

About eleven, Mrs. Grant, seeing he was in great pain from pressure and coldness in his breast and arms, called Sarah Jane, who was upstairs. As she came down I entered the house. It was evident that the attack was serious and dangerous. Uncle prayed that his sufferings might be short and that he might soon be at rest...

Miss Grant got the remedies which usually relieved him. They gradually relieved the pain but his head and face remained as cold as death. He had no more pain. His voice continued natural and strong and his head clear until he died about an hour after the attack began.

He was cheerful, kind, and friendly and affectionate. He said he was glad I could be with him. I held his right hand. He said, 'John Rogers probably suffered more than I have, but he didn't make so much fuss as I do.' 'You, as a soldier wounded, were worse off than I, but you were a hero and could bear it.' 'I shall soon see Fanny and Mrs. Valette; that is, if I go to the right place (this with a playful smile) and I think I shall.' And so with pleasant talk until the moment when a single spasm brought the end. A beautiful close to a beautiful life."

AUGUST 28, 1874, SPIEGEL GROVE, FREMONT, OHIO,
DEATH OF SON MANNING FORCE

Little Manning died on his mother's forty-third birthday.

"August 28, Friday, A.M.—Our dear little Manning died this morning soon after midnight, about 12:30. He suffered very little, being wholly unconscious the last hour or two. He has not seemed altogether healthy at any time…He was a lovely, beautiful child. His eyes were very dark, large, mild, and sweet. His forehead broad, high, and prominent. Probably our handsomest child except Georgey. Dear boy! he is lost to us. We may hope he is saved from a world of suffering and sorrow."

OCTOBER 12, 1875, FREMONT, OHIO, ELECTED GOVERNOR, THIRD TERM

Imagine any current presidential candidate, let alone governor, letting slip the following:

"Fremont, Ohio, June 8, 1875,

My Dear Major: —At any rate, being on the track, I now want to win, and am willing to do my share of the solid work required to do it. It is of the first importance to nominate in the counties, and [to] organize early.

For the topics of the canvass, and bringing them before the people, the press is the means. Meetings and speeches are less important relatively than ever before. They come in too late, and in a day of enterprising newspaper men, they are merely stale repetitions of the press. Meetings and speeches, like the election itself, are the results of what the press has already done.

…What I have said about meetings and speeches is not with a view to shirk labor. I am ready to do all that may be reasonably expected. But early and earnest discussion by the press is, I am sure, far more effective.

Sincerely,

R. B. Hayes"

Once again, and despite the use of an exclamation point in the first sentence, Hayes prepared himself for defeat, and predicted the coming swarm of presidential king-makers.

"October 12, 1875—Election day! The weather is perfect. Spiegel Grove, my home, never looked so beautiful before. I am as nearly indifferent, on personal grounds, to the result of this day as it is possible to be. I prefer success. But I anticipate defeat with very great equanimity.

If victorious, I am likely to be pushed for the Republican nomination for president. This would make my life a disturbed and troubled one until the nomination, six or eight months hence. If nominated, the stir would last until November a year hence. Defeat in the next presidential election is almost a certainty. In any event, defeat now returns me to the quiet life I sought in coming here.

"I go to Toledo to meet with Centennial State Board today. I am asked to speak on Decoration Day in Toledo. I am inclined to accept. May I speak of uniting with Confederates in this ceremony?

I would honor any man who dies in obedience to his convictions of duty, who dies for others. The conductor, the engineer, the brakeman, who dies at his post; the captain, the sailor who goes down at sea to save his passengers; the fireman who perishes, the policeman who is killed in the line of duty. But how of those who died in an effort to destroy the good? Does he believe in his work?

—*Hayes, diary, May 11, 1875*

The large considerations of country, patriotism, and principle find little place in a deliberation on this question. The march of events will carry us safely beyond the dangers of the present questions."

No exclamation point for the result, possibly as he reflected out his library window at Spiegel Grove knowing he was headed back to Columbus.

"October 17, 1875—Elected. A pleasant serenade from my neighbors; a day of doubt and anxiety as to the result. It looked on Thursday as if the Democrats were bent on counting me out. All right, however. Now come papers from all the country counties urging me for the Presidential nomination."

Indeed, they were coming. In less than a year's time, Rutherford Hayes would be inaugurated for an unprecedented third term as governor of Ohio, win the Republican nomination for president, and be launched into the first congressionally contested election since Jackson-Adams in 1824.

November 7, 1876, Columbus, Ohio, Election Day

The election of 1876 has been covered in a plethora of scholarly works. For the purpose of this book, the story of his election in November begins back in June at the convention:

"June 16, 1876. Friday, 8 A. M.—This is the third day of the convention at Cincinnati. My friends were there a week ago tonight. One whole week of convention work. At the adjournment last night, all was ready to begin the balloting. At ten this morning the decisive balloting begins. Early in the struggle, my friends were very hopeful. But on the 13th, Blaine became decidedly the prominent man—his prospects deemed almost a

RUTHERFORD B. HAYES.

Hayes circa 1876.

certainty. There has been a gradual change on the 14th and 15th, and now it seems something more than a possibility that he will fail.

If he fails, my chance, as a compromise candidate, seems to be better than that of any other candidate. So, we are now in suspense. I have kept cool and unconcerned to a degree that surprises me. The same may be said of Lucy. I feel that defeat will be a great relief—a setting free from bondage.

The great responsibility overpowers me. That is too strong. It sobers me. It is a weight, but not overpowering. I shall try to do in all things, more than ever before, if nominated, precisely the thing that is right, to be natural, discreet, wise, moderate, and as firm in the right as it is possible for me to be. And in this spirit I await the event!

Sunday, June 18—I have had no time to write since my nomination, on the seventh ballot, about 4 P. M. on the 16th, Friday. Friday has been a lucky day for me before. My deepest emotions were on receiving Blaine's dispatch of congratulation. It for a few moments quite unmanned me. And then Shoemaker's dispatch, wishing that Uncle Birchard was alive."

In his acceptance address, Hayes put forth a pledge which many historians (and pundits and talking heads) forget he proposed before he was elected. Hayes offered the unthinkable—to serve only one term. Only Hayes could consider such an unselfish idea, and he wrote to one of the leaders of Civil Service Reform to bounce the idea around:

"To Carl Schurz: Columbus, Ohio, June 27, 1876,

One other suggestion, let me now submit to you: I really think that a president could do more good in one term if untrammeled by the belief that he was fixing things for his election to a second term, than with the best intentions could be done in two terms with his power embarrassed by that suspicion or temptation during his first four years. Our platform

— RUTHERFORD HAYES —

says nothing on the subject. I am averse to adding topics, but could I not properly avow my own view and purpose on this head?"

The election was exhausting. His opponent, Samuel Tilden of New York, was a formidable candidate and Hayes rightly sensed it was going to be a Democratic year. There could be no 'bloody shirt' waving (the Republicans tired use of Civil War memories to elect candidates), and once and for all, the country was tired of Reconstruction.

Hayes was tired, too. To Lucy he wrote:

"August 13, 1876,

When I am alone I always wish I was a quiet private citizen again. But it will soon be if we are beaten. I almost hope we shall be. Independence is such a comfort and blessing.

As ever, R."

Election Day was held on November 7, 1876. Hayes predicted a loss:

"Columbus, November 7, 1876—Dies irae [Latin for Day of Wrath] —A cold but dry day. Good enough here for election work. I still think Democratic chances the best. But it is not possible to form a confident opinion. If we lose, the South will be the greatest sufferer. Their misfortune will be far greater than ours. I do not think a revival of business will be greatly postponed by Tilden's election. Business prosperity does not, in my judgment, depend on government so much as men commonly think. But we shall have no improvement in civil service—deterioration rather, and the South will drift towards chaos again."

Tilden won the popular vote with 4,288,546 total votes to Hayes 4,034,311. The electoral college was another matter, with disputed votes in Florida, Oregon, and Louisiana. Both candidates' 'camps' claimed the disputed states, and the answer would hang in the wind like dandelion chaff, unwilling to land, content to float from one acre to the next.

Founders had set Inauguration Day on the fourth of March so that the new president would have time, if necessary, to travel from pioneer states. Little did they know on the centennial of the Revolution, every one of those days would be needed just to sort the mess out.

"Saturday, November 11, 1876,

All thoughtful people are brought to consider the imperfect machinery provided for electing the President. No doubt we shall, warned by this danger, provide, by amendments of the Constitution, or by proper legislation, against a recurrence of the danger."

By the way…we did not.

November 27, 1876, Columbus, Ohio,
"There must be nothing crooked on our part."

The honor, duty, and loyal dedication of Rutherford Hayes did not change on Election Day when the votes were cast and he was presumed defeated. The following excerpts prove his line of thinking during the election chaos that followed the disputed electoral votes. That somehow the legacy of Hayes is tarnished, still in the modern era, by the treachery which was not within his reach or by his bidding, is one of many tragedies of history.

And his thinking began well before the election:

"Columbus, October 22, 1876, Sunday—Only two Sundays more before the Presidential election. I am surprised, whenever I think of it, to find myself so cool, so almost indifferent about it. It would be a calamity,

I am sure, to give the Democrats the Government. But public opinion, the press, the march of events, will compel them to do better than their character and principles indicate. Here is our safety. Public opinion, the fear of losing the public confidence, apprehension of censure by the press, make all men in power conservative and safe.

On personal grounds, I find many reasons for thinking defeat a blessing. I should stand by my Letter, I should hew to the line; but what conflicts and annoyances would follow! I do not fear my pluck or constancy a particle. But to be deceived by the rogues, to find many a trusted reformer no better than he should be, here would be humiliations and troubles without end.

The huge registration in New York City looks sinister. It seems to look to our defeat in that State. Another danger is imminent: A contested result. And we have no such means for its decision as ought to be provided by law. This must be attended to hereafter. We should not allow another Presidential election to occur before a means for settling a contest is provided. If a contest comes now it may lead to a conflict of arms. I can only try to do my duty to my countrymen in that case. I shall let no personal ambition turn me from the path of duty. Bloodshed and civil war must be averted if possible. If forced to fight, I have no fears of failure from lack of courage or firmness."

After the dispute began, Hayes had it spelled out in his diary, but, as usual, found peace in defeat:

"Sunday, November 12, 1876—We shall, the fair-minded men of the country will, history will hold that the Republicans were by fraud, violence, and intimidation, by a nullification of the Fifteenth Amendment, deprived of the victory which they fairly won. But we must, I now think, prepare ourselves to accept the inevitable. I do it with composure and cheerfulness. To me the result is no personal calamity."

Some have suggested Hayes was working behind the scenes to win the dispute. Hayes wrote to John Sherman to erase any doubt:

"Columbus, Ohio, November 27, 1876,

My Dear Sir: —I am greatly obliged for your letter of the 23d. You feel, I am sure, as I do about this whole business. A fair election would have given us about forty electoral votes at the South—at least that many. But we are not to allow our friends to defeat one outrage and fraud by another. There must be nothing crooked on our part. Let Mr. Tilden have the place by violence, intimidation, and fraud, rather than undertake to prevent it by means that will not bear the severest scrutiny.

I appreciate the work doing by the Republicans who have gone South and am especially proud of the acknowledged honorable conduct of those from Ohio. The Democrats made a mistake in sending so many ex-Republicans. New converts are proverbially bitter and unfair towards those they have recently left.

I trust you will soon reach the end of the work, and be able to return in health and safety.

Sincerely,

R. B. Hayes"

It was decided an electoral commission should award the electoral votes of Florida, Oregon, and Louisiana. Seven Democrats, seven Republicans, and one independent Justice of the Supreme Court would decide. During the run up to the vote, the Justice (David Davis of Illinois) accepted a seat in the Senate and had to be replaced.

"Friday, January 26, 1877—I have not tried to influence the opinions or actions of anybody on the bill. Before another Presidential election, this whole subject of the Presidential election ought to be thoroughly considered, and a radical change made. It is probable that no wise measure can be devised which does not require an amendment of the Constitution. Let proposed amendments be maturely considered. Something ought to be done immediately."

—Hayes, diary

When the new judge was announced, it was son Webb who happily broke the news to his father:

"Columbus, January 31, 1877—The Commission seems to be a good one. At 2 P.M. Webb announced, 'The judge—it is Bradley. In Washington the bets are five to one that the next [President] will be Hayes.'

But I am in no way elated. I prefer success. But I am clear that for our happiness failure is to be preferred. I shall, therefore, await the event with the utmost composure. If the result is adverse, I shall be cheerful, quiet, and serene. If successful, may God give me grace to be firm and wise and just—clear in the great office—for the true interest of all the people of the United States!"

Hayes was notified of his election on March 2, 1877, two days before his Inauguration.

President...

MARCH 5, 1877, WASHINGTON, DC, INAUGURATION

We can only imagine the flood of emotions Hayes held back on March 5, 1877, as he waited on the platform in front of the United States Capitol Building, where every president since Jefferson had stood to take the oath of office. The Kenyon Man, the Harvard Man, the Fighting Man—who bravely suffered through as many wounds as years in service. The governor of Ohio, who three times had been elected and three times he challenged his fellow statesmen to embrace the mantel of Lincoln and "malice toward none, and charity for all."

Hayes life was epitomized in the future epitaph of Theodore Roosevelt's "Man in the Arena":

"It is not the critic who counts; not the man who points out how the strong man stumbles, or where the doer of deeds could have done them better. The credit belongs to the man who is actually in the arena, whose face is marred by dust and sweat and blood; who strives valiantly; who errs, who comes short again and again, because there is no effort without error and shortcoming; but who does actually strive to do the deeds; who knows great enthusiasms, the great devotions; who spends himself in a worthy cause; who at the best knows in the end the triumph of high achievement, and who at the worst, if he fails, at least fails while daring greatly, so that his place shall never be with those cold and timid souls who neither know victory nor defeat."[1]

Surely, this was a man, standing "so at ease"[2] according to biographer Harry Barnard, who had reached the pinnacle of power in the United States by doing his duty with honor and dignity. As he said in his diary in November 1872, "Do what is natural to you, and you are sure to get all the recognition you are entitled to."

The Hayes Inaugural Address was brief and succinct, as Hayes always preferred.

Excerpted here is the important question of the South. Hayes had promised to remove troops from southern states, effectively ending Reconstruction. But Hayes also realized it was not the end. His call towards the South is as worthy of our attention as Lincoln's Inaugural in 1861:

"Many of the calamitous efforts of the tremendous revolution which has passed over the Southern States still remain. The immeasurable benefits which will surely follow, sooner or later, the hearty and generous acceptance of the legitimate results of that revolution have not yet been realized. Difficult and embarrassing questions meet us at the threshold of this subject. The people of those States are still impoverished, and the inestimable blessing of wise, honest, and peaceful local self-government is not fully enjoyed. Whatever difference of opinion may exist as to the cause of this condition of things, the fact is clear that in the progress of events the time has come when such government is the imperative necessity required by all the varied interests, public and private, of those States. But it must not be forgotten that only a local government which recognizes and maintains inviolate the rights of all is a true self-government.

With respect to the two distinct races whose peculiar relations to each other have brought upon us the deplorable complications and perplexities which exist in those States, it must be a government which guards the interests of both races carefully and equally. It must be a government which submits loyally and heartily to the Constitution and the laws—the laws of the nation and the laws of the States themselves—accepting and obeying faithfully the whole Constitution as it is.

Resting upon this sure and substantial foundation, the superstructure of beneficent local governments can be built

Hayes inauguration, 1877.

up, and not otherwise. In furtherance of such obedience to the letter and the spirit of the Constitution, and in behalf of all that its attainment implies, all so-called party interests lose their apparent importance, and party lines may well be permitted to fade into insignificance. The question we have to consider for the immediate welfare of those States of the Union is the question of government or no government; of social order and all the peaceful industries and the happiness that belongs to it, or a return to barbarism. It is a question in which every citizen of the nation is deeply interested, and with respect to which we ought not to be, in a partisan sense, either Republicans or Democrats, but fellow-citizens and fellowmen, to whom the interests of a common country and a common humanity are dear.

The sweeping revolution of the entire labor system of a large portion of our country and the advance of 4,000,000 people from a condition of servitude to that of citizenship, upon an equal footing with their former masters, could not occur without presenting problems of the gravest moment, to be dealt with by the emancipated race, by their former masters, and by the General Government, the author of the act of emancipation. That it was a wise, just, and providential act, fraught with good for all concerned, is not generally conceded throughout the country. That a moral obligation rests upon the National Government to employ its constitutional power and influence to establish the rights of the people it has emancipated, and to protect them in the enjoyment of those rights when they are infringed or assailed, is also generally admitted.

The evils which afflict the Southern States can only be removed or remedied by the united and harmonious efforts of both races, actuated by motives of mutual sympathy and regard; and while in duty bound and fully determined to protect the rights of all by every constitutional means at the disposal of my Administration, I am sincerely anxious to use every legitimate influence in favor of honest and efficient local self-government as the true resource of those States for the promotion of the contentment and prosperity of their citizens. In the effort I shall make to accomplish this purpose I ask the cordial cooperation of all who cherish an interest in the welfare of the country, trusting that party ties and the prejudice of race will be freely surrendered in behalf of the great purpose to be accomplished. In the important work of restoring the South it is not the political situation alone that merits attention. The material development of that section of the country has been arrested by the social and political revolution through which it has passed, and now needs and deserves the considerate care of the National Government within the just limits prescribed by the Constitution and wise public economy.

But at the basis of all prosperity, for that as well as for every other part of the country, lies the improvement of the intellectual and moral condition of the people. Universal suffrage should rest upon universal education. To this end, liberal and permanent provision should be made for the support of free schools by the State governments, and, if need be, supplemented by legitimate aid from national authority.

Let me assure my countrymen of the Southern States that it is my earnest desire to regard and promote their truest interest—the interests of the white and of the colored people both and equally—and to put forth my best efforts in behalf of a civil policy which will forever wipe out in our political affairs the color line and the distinction between North and South, to the end that we may have not merely a united North or a united South, but a united country."[3]

Hayes went on to call for major reforms of the Civil Service, (using his oft-quoted phrase that, "He serves his party best who serves the country best") a one-term president of six years in length, paper currency dependent on coin, and a Constitutional Amendment requiring an overhaul of the Electoral College system.

It was a lot to do, in a very short amount of time.

1.   "Citizenship in A Republic," Theodore Roosevelt, April 23, 1910, Sorbonne, Paris, France.

2.   Barnard, Harry, *Rutherford Hayes and His America*, (Newtown, Connecticut, Bobbs Merrill Company, 1954) 399.

3.   "Inaugural Address of Rutherford Hayes," Avalon.law.yale.edu.

MARCH 8, 1877, WASHINGTON DC, STANDING FIRM ON APPOINTMENTS

Rutherford Hayes could not afford to follow in the footsteps of Abraham Lincoln and appoint men to his cabinet whom he had defeated for the nomination. As well, there was not the caliber of men in 1877 as there was in 1861. Even before he was assured of his victory, he began making notes in his diary:

"February 19 [Diary]—For Cabinet:

1.   A new Cabinet—no member of the present.

2.   No Presidential candidates.

3.   No appointment to "take care" of anybody.

Saturday and Sunday saw Senators and Representatives and others, and many suggestions on the Cabinet. Blaine urged Fry. Hamlin much vexed and grieved when I told him I couldn't appoint Fry. Blaine seemed to claim it, as a condition of good relations with me. Cameron and Logan greatly urged all day. I told Cameron I could not appoint him. Too many of the old Cabinet had good claims to remain, to recognize one without appointing more than would be advisable. I accordingly nominated:

Wm. M. Evarts, New York, State,

John Sherman, Ohio, Treasury,

Carl Schurz, Missouri, Interior,

General Charles Devens, Massachusetts, Attorney-General,

D. M. Key, Tennessee, Postmaster-General,

George W. McCrary, Iowa, War,

R. W. Thompson, Indiana, Navy."

For three days, Hayes stood firm as senator after senator, congressman after congressman filed through his office with complaints either on behalf of someone else or, in the case of powerful senators like Roscoe Conkling and James Blaine, for themselves. For a new president, who assumed office under the extraordinary circumstances which Hayes did, it was like a sparrow in a hurricane. But Hayes persevered, as he had with his midnight callers four years prior.

In the end, the public had their say. Hayes recorded in his diary, "After a few days the public opinion of the country was shown by the press to be strongly with me. All of the nominations were confirmed by almost a unanimous vote."

Once again, Hayes stood firm on his principles and came out in the right. It was a good start to his administration, and he desperately needed it.

MARCH 15, 1877, WASHINGTON, DC,
NOMINATION OF FREDERICK DOUGLASS PROVOST OF DC

President Hayes was immediately tasked with a myriad of contentious issues, all focusing on the treatment of the two factions in the South left aching for their rights as "new" Americans. Both southern whites and southern blacks needed their assurances, both in legislation and in rhetoric. Hayes knew this, and walked the edge of the cliff with the confidence that, at least perhaps literally, he had been there before. He wrote in his diary on March 16:

"Stanley Matthews was yesterday night nominated for Senator at Columbus. This is an endorsement of the policy of peace and home rule-of local self-government. A number of Southern Republican members are reported ready to go over to the Democrats. On the other hand, the bar of this District [of Columbia] are in a state of mind because Fred Douglass, the most distinguished and able colored man in the

Nation, has been nominated marshal for the District.

If a liberal policy towards late Rebels is adopted, the ultra Republicans are opposed to it; if the colored people are honored, the extremists of the other wing cry out against it. I suspect I am right in both cases."

The appointment, however high in significance, was not without controversy, unintended by the president. The Marshal-Provost was to be at the side of the president during all formal occasions. For this position, the president sincerely wanted his son (and Secretary) Webb.

Later that year, he continued to encourage others in his administration to follow his lead and appoint qualified African Americans. Writing to John King, the Collector of New Orleans:

"Private.

Executive Mansion, Washington DC, May 7, 1877,

Dear Sir: The appointment of colored men to places under you for which they are qualified, will tend to secure to people of their race consideration and will diminish race prejudice. Other elements of your population are, of course, not to be overlooked. Please consult with Colonel Wharton and endeavor to arrange your subordinate appointments so as to harmonize and meet the wishes and approval of all classes of good citizens, and at the same time to promote the efficiency of the service.

Sincerely,

R. B. Hayes"

APRIL 3, 1877, WASHINGTON, DC, HAYES ORDERS TROOPS OUT OF SOUTH CAROLINA.

Casual readers of history of this period, often uninterested in the back and forth of the Reconstruction Era, look at a headline about "Troops Removed from Capitol" and may assume the number to be in the thousands. Correction: According to biographer Harry Barnard, there were nineteen. Nineteen soldiers in the South Carolina capitol building in Columbia.

Nonetheless, South Carolina wanted them out and President Hayes, after dutiful research on the subject, came to the conclusion to follow through with his promise:

"March 23—It is not the duty of the President of the United States to use the military power of the Nation to decide contested elections in the States. He will maintain the authority of the United States and keep the peace between the contending parties. But local self-government means the determination by each State for itself of all questions as to its own local affairs.

The real thing to be achieved is safety and prosperity for the colored people. Both houses of Congress and the public opinion of the country are plainly against the use of the army to uphold either claimant to the State Government in case of contest. The wish is to restore harmony and good feeling between sections and races. This can only be done by peaceful methods.

We wish to adjust the difficulties in Louisiana and South Carolina so as to make one government out of two in each State. But if this fails, if no adjustment can be made, we must then adopt the non-intervention policy, except so far as may be necessary to keep the peace.

April 22—We have got through with the South Carolina and Louisiana [problems]. At any rate, the troops are ordered away, and I now hope for peace, and what is equally important, security and prosperity for the colored people. The result of my plans is to get from those States by their governors, legislatures, press, and people pledges that the Thirteenth, Fourteenth, and Fifteenth Amendments shall be faithfully observed; that the colored people shall have equal rights to labor, education, and the privileges of citizenship. I am confident this is a good work. Time will tell.

Now for civil service reform. Legislation must be prepared and executive rules and maxims. We must limit and narrow the area of patronage. We must diminish the evils of office-seeking. We must stop interference of federal officers with elections. We must be relieved of congressional dictation as to appointments."

President Hayes wrote, "Time will tell." It would not be until the Civil Rights Act of 1965 that African American's would be guaranteed the right to vote unimpeded by taxes, tests, and outright murder.

AUGUST 19, 1877, WASHINGTON, DC,

THE BAN ON ALCOHOL IN THE EXECUTIVE MANSION

If Rutherford Hayes was made for the moment in 1877, so too was his wife Lucy. Modest, religious, and reserved, on her very first day as the wife of the president, on the platform listening to his inaugural address, she conducted herself in such a manner to win over the immediate respect and admiration of a respected female reporter named Mary Clemmer Ames.[1]

Ames, on the very day she watched the inauguration, and specifically watched Lucy, coined the phrase "First Lady of the Land." The term stuck, and not just because Ames wrote it and others followed her lead. It stuck because Lucy filled the term with honesty, grace, and dignity just by being herself.

She was the first "First Lady" but she was also the first to invite the scorn of certain members of the republic like no one since Mrs. Abraham Lincoln. It happened quickly after the visit of Grand Duke Alexis of Russia. Six glasses of wine were served with the meal dedicated to, as all state dinners, honor the hosts and their country. President Hayes and the First Lady did not drink the wine, and soon thereafter the president banned alcohol from being served in the executive mansion completely.[2] Those in the anti-Temperance movement forever after referred to the First Lady as "Lemonade Lucy." It was not a term of endearment.

There were, as always in politics, two reasons for such a pronouncement. The ban satisfied the first lady, it satisfied the temperance movement, but it also, according to Hayes, cooled the frustrations of a faction of the Republicans yearning to break apart and form a radical political party with one mission: Prohibition. Hayes, rightly so, felt they could kill multiple birds with one stone, even if it meant inviting the scorn of a few.

After Representative Garfield was elected president, Hayes recorded the following views on his policy in the president's home:

"Sunday, January 16, 1881,

It is said General Garfield will restore wine and liquor to the White House. I hope this is a mistake. I am no fanatic on this subject. I do not sympathize with the methods of the ultra-temperance people. I believe that the cause of temperance will be most surely promoted by moral, religious, and educational influences and by the influence of example.

I would not use the force of law as an agency for temperance reform. If laws on the subject are enacted, let them be for the security of the community, to protect the public from nuisances and crime. Let the temperance reformer keep to the text, influence, argument, persuasion, example.

When we came here we banished liquors from the house—

1. Because it was right, wise, and necessary.
2. Because it was due to the large support given me by the sincere friends of the temperance reform.
3. Because I believed that it would strengthen the Republican party by detaching from the political Temperance party many good people who would join the Republican party [and] would save to the Republican party many who would otherwise leave it to join the Temperance party.

If General Garfield rejects the practice I have inaugurated, he will offend thousands, and drive them into the hands of the temperance demagogues. He will lose the confidence of thousands of good citizens and gain no strength in any quarter. His course will be taken as evidence that he lacks the grit to face fashionable ridicule. Nothing hurts a man more than a general belief that he lacks 'the courage of his convictions.'"

On this platform no one, even in 1877, would argue, Hayes was not having the courage of his convictions.

1. Geer, *First Lady, The Life of Lucy Webb Hayes*, 138.

2. Geer, *First Lady, The Life of Lucy Webb Hayes*, 148.

JULY 18, 1877, SOLDIER'S HOME, WASHINGTON, DC,
ENDING THE GREAT RAIL STRIKE

Railroads were the pulse of the nation in 1877, and supplying the pulse were the hundreds of thousands of railroad workers making sure the trains were on track and on time. Behind the workers were the owners of the railroads who slowly but surely lowered wages to less than $1.50 a day.[1]

The worker's frustrations boiled over in July, and a strike was called, first in Martinsburg, West Virginia, and then spread nationally to Baltimore, and as far as California. Tempers flared across the major cities as strikers refused to either return to work or go home. Fighting broke out in Pittsburgh, Columbus, and Chicago. Men were killed and governors became frantic, calling on President Hayes to roll out the militia.[2]

Hayes studied his role, conferred with his cabinet and finally decided the militia could be used but under strict orders to simply, as his oath allowed, 'protect' property and citizens. The mere presence of the militia poured cold water on the heated cities. Hayes had thwarted a major crisis that some believed had the potential for open revolution.[3]

Hayes reflected on the situation in August at the soldier's home, a cottage three miles north of the executive mansion where Lincoln had spent a quarter of his presidency. For the record, Hayes uses the word "force" to describe the cause for the end of the strike, but there was no armed "force" as we may assume in modern society. "Force" was simply the presence of troops.

"August 5. Sunday, Soldiers' Home—

The strikes have been put down by force; but now for the real remedy. Can't something [be] done by education of the strikers, by judicious control of the capitalists, by wise general policy to end or diminish the evil? The railroad strikers, as a rule, are good men, sober, intelligent, and industrious. The mischiefs are:

1. Strikers prevent men willing to work from doing so.
2. They seize and hold the property of their employers.
3. The consequent excitement furnishes an opportunity for the dangerous criminal classes to destroy life and property.
- Now, 'every man has a right, if he sees fit to, to quarrel with his own bread and butter, but he has no right to quarrel with the bread and butter of other people.'
- Every man has a right to determine for himself the value of his own labor, but he has no right to determine for other men the value of their labor. (Not good.)
- Every man has a right to refuse to work if the wages don't suit him, but he has no right to prevent others from working if they are suited with the wages.
- Every man has a right to refuse to work, but no man has a right to prevent others from working.
- Every man has a right to decide for himself the question of wages, but no man has a right to decide that question for other men."

Hayes was fortunate the militia righted the ship, but also fortunate no one on either side allowed a cross word or sudden motion to spark an outburst that would have put President Hayes right back in the line of fire.

1. Barnard, *Rutherford B. Hayes and His America*, 445.

2. Ibid.

3. Ibid.

SEPTEMBER 22, 1877, ATLANTA, GEORGIA, ADDRESS TO A MIXED AUDIENCE

President Obama was the first president to utilize the internet and social media to talk directly to the people. President Kennedy was the first president to utilize television. President Franklin Roosevelt was the first to utilize radio.

President Hayes was the first president to utilize the railroad.

He traveled extensively, enjoying the warmth of the crowds and meeting the citizens of a country split among so many different factions and creeds.

Where did the president who ended reconstruction head in the fall of his first year? Into the south, as deep as Atlanta where he was the first president to address a mixed audience. Just as he faced Jubal Early head on, he spoke directly to the issues confronting audience members who were practically shoulder to shoulder with a different race.

"And here we are, Republicans, Democrats, colored people, white people, Confederate soldiers and Union soldiers, all of one mind and one heart today. And why should we not be? What is there to separate us longer? Without any fault of yours or any fault of mine, or of any one of this great audience, slavery existed in this country. It was in the Constitution of the country.

The colored man was here, not by his own voluntary action. It was a misfortune of his fathers he was here, and I think it is safe to say it was by a crime of our fathers he was here. He was here, however, and we of the two sections differed about what should be done with him. As Mr. Lincoln told us in the war, there were prayers on both sides for him; both sides found Bible confirmation of their opinions, and both sides finally undertook to settle the question by that last final means of arbitration—force of arms.

You here mainly joined the Confederate side, and fought bravely, and risked your lives heroically in behalf of your convictions, and can any true man anywhere fail to respect a man who risks his life for his convictions? And as I accord that respect to you and believe you to be equally liberal and generous and just, I feel as I stand before you as one who fought in the Union army for his own convictions, I am entitled to your respect...

...Then, my friends, we are all together upon one proposition. We believe—and in this all those who are here agree—in the Union of our fathers, in the flag of our fathers, the Constitution as it is, with all the amendments, and are prepared to see it fully and fairly obeyed and enforced.

Now, my friends, I see it stated occasionally that President Hayes has taken the course he has because he was compelled to. Now, I was compelled to it. I was compelled to it by my sense of duty under my oath of office. What was done by us was done not merely by force of special circumstances, but because we believed it just and right to do it.

Now let us come together; let each man make up his mind to be a patriot in his own home and place. You may quarrel about tariff, get up sharp contests about currency, about the removal of the State Capitols, and where they shall go to; but upon the great question of the union of the States and the rights of all citizens, we shall agree forevermore.

I shall not forget this reception and this greeting. Every good purpose I have will be strengthened by what I have seen and heard today. I thank you for the help it will give me hereafter during my term of office. I bid you good morning."

Abraham Lincoln would have been proud.

OCTOBER 6, 1877, WASHINGTON, DC, ELECTED TO PEABODY FUND

Hayes fervently believed the next logical step after emancipation achieved under Lincoln and assured by the constitution was education. And he committed his time and money to the cause, beginning with his election as trustee to the Peabody Fund, a 3.4-million-dollar endowment left by George Peabody for the sole purpose of the destruction of illiteracy in African Americans and caucasians in the South.[1]

"Sunday, October 7, 1877, Soldiers' Home—

Lucy returned yesterday morning from New York. The nomination by the southern members of the Peabody [Education Fund] Trustees and the unanimous election by the whole board are agreeable things. They prove that the pacification measures are approved by the whole country. It is also an exceedingly honorable and pleasant employment."

1. Hoogenboom, *Rutherford B. Hayes, Warrior and President,* 317.

DECEMBER 30, 1877, EXECUTIVE MANSION, WASHINGTON, DC, THE SILVER WEDDING ANNIVERSARY

There were happy times in the president's house. Long before the Roosevelt children rode their ponies into the Executive Mansion, the Hayes' two youngest children, Scott and Fanny, roamed the halls. Scott loved the goat cart that pulled the boy across the White House lawn and both children accompanied their parents on official business. Fanny helped Lucy decorate the graves of Civil War soldiers at

October 4, 1877

"I must resolve on this birthday to do better in
the future than ever before. With good health
and great opportunities, may I not hope to
confer great and lasting benefits on my country?
I mean to try. Let me be kind and considerate
in treatment of the unfortunate who crowd my
doorway, and firm and conscientious in dealing
with the tempters. The Southern question
seems to be on a good footing. The currency
also. The Mexican question is perplexing.
The improvement of the civil service, I must
constantly labor for."

Arlington National Cemetery, and Scott was introduced to his father's important guests.[1]

The Hayes' second son, Webb, served as his father's secretary. Margaret Truman records a humorous anecdote about Webb in her collection of White House stories in her book, *The President's House*. Webb's final daily duty was locking the doors of the Executive Mansion. After receptions when guests would inevitably linger and his parents had long since retired, Webb would be anxious to go to bed himself. Apparently he arranged to have a large object dropped, quieting the room (and jarring the guests). Someone would inevitably note the time and suggest going home.[2]

On December 30, 1877, Rutherford and Lucy celebrated twenty-five years of marriage by renewing their vows in the Blue Room. Lucy wore her wedding dress, and even held the same hand of Laura Platt Mitchell as she had when the girl, Rutherford's niece, stood beside her in Cincinnati twenty-five years previous.[3]

The Hayes marriage was strong, and their bond is still remembered today with the annual White House Easter Egg Roll. According to Truman, the event was previously held on the grounds of the Capitol Building until 1878 when public events were outlawed on the Capitol grounds. The kids showed up anyway, and were headed to the Executive Mansion where Rutherford and Lucy Hayes welcomed them with open arms.[4]

1.   Truman, Margaret, *The President's House*, (New York, Ballantine, 2003), 245.

2.   Truman, *The President's House*, 103.

3.   Geer, *First Lady, The Life of Lucy Webb Hayes*, 174.

4.   Truman, *The President's House*, 246.

July 11, 1878, Washington, DC, Hayes Fires
Chester Alan Arthur and Cornell

"Nothing brings out the lower traits of human nature like office-seeking. Men of good character and impulses are betrayed by it into all sorts of meanness. Disappointment makes them unjust to the last degree."

—Hayes, diary, August 9, 1878

If the 45th Congress was a school at recess, Roscoe Conkling was the bully by the swing set, frightening children and getting his way through fear and intimidation. Conkling, the powerful senator from New York State, looked and acted much like a peacock, strutting and gesturing to summon attention and constantly forward his schemes without regard for anyone but himself. His agenda, much of the time, involved rewarding his friends and allies with jobs.

One of those allies was a man named Chester Alan Arthur. The long line of presidential succession will soon record Arthur's name on the list of chief executives, but in 1878, he was Chief Collector of the New York Customhouse. In charge of an army of government employees numbering in the thousands, Arthur was steadfastly devoted to his "boss," Senator Conkling, for his position, which paid a salary grossly inflated due to corruption and payoffs. In the eras before Hayes, employees of the customhouse—and all government positions for that matter—were hired on the basis of political party. Politicians like Conkling could also demand contributions from employees and require loyalty oaths, all processes Hayes was determined to end.

As he recorded earlier in his administration:

"August 5, 1877, Soldier's Home,

I grow more conservative every day on the question of removals. On ex parte statements, I have made mistakes in removing men who, perhaps, ought to have been retained, and in appointing wrong men. Not many removals have been made. Less than by any new Administration since John Q. Adams. But I shall be more cautious in future; make

Washington, February 16, 1878.

Dear Sir:— The only American whose birthday is generally known and widely celebrated is Washington. The Father of his Country is remembered and honored throughout the world for what he did, and what he was.

None of my young friends who read this patriotic number of the *Sunday School Times* are likely to have an opportunity to do such great deeds as were done by Washington, but all of them will have an opportunity to be like him in character.

They can have his love of country, his integrity, and his firmness in doing the right. To have such a character is better than rank, or wealth, or fame. It is a possession which can't be taken away.

As Webster said so impressively of 'a sense of duty,' 'It will be with us through this life, will be with us at its close, and in that scene of inconceivable solemnity which lies yet farther onward,' it will still be with us.

Sincerely,

R. B. Hayes

—To H. Clay Trumbull,
Editor of the Sunday School Times

removals only in clear cases, and appoint men only on the best and fullest evidence of fitness.

There are some points on which good men, North and South, are agreed—generally are agreed—for it is not given to men that all good men should be agreed on any question relating to public affairs.

1. We agree that it is not well that political parties should be formed on sectional lines.
2. That it is not well that parties should divide on color lines.
3. That we should not divide on any line or principle of division which inevitably leads to (contest) conflict, which can only be settled by the bayonet.

October 24, 1877—It is now obvious that there is a very decided opposition to the Administration, in both houses of Congress, among the Republican members. There seems not to be any considerable personal hostility to me. But a conference of about twenty members of the House at Mr. Sherman's developed a decided hostility to my measures on the part of members, respectable both in character and number. The objections extend to all of my principal acts. This opposition is directed against:

1. The Cabinet—It is said there are only four Republican members, viz., Sherman, Devens, McCrary, and Thompson. That Evarts and Schurz are disorganizers, doctrinaires, and liberals, and Key is a Democrat.
2. The attempt to make the civil service non-partisan is ruinous to the party, unjust and oppressive to office-holders, and is an attempt to accomplish the impossible, viz., a non-partisan civil service.
3. The pacification of the South is a total departure from the principles, traditions, and wishes of the party. A majority of members probably favor some part of these measures. Only a small number support all of them. The adversary points to the results of elections, as showing that the people condemn the Administration, and that it is destroying the party.

4. The most bitter opposition arises from the apprehension that the course of the Administration will deprive Congressmen of all control and share of the patronage of the Government.

How to meet and overcome this opposition is the question. I am clear that I am right. I believe that a large majority of the best people are in full accord with me. Now, my purpose is to keep cool; to treat all adversaries considerately, respectfully, and kindly, but at the same time in a way to satisfy them of my sincerity and firmness. In all parts of my official conduct to strive conscientiously and unselfishly to do what is wise.

In my anxiety to complete the great work of pacification, I have neglected to give due attention to the civil service—to the appointments and removals. The result is, some bad appointments have been made. Some removals have been mistakes. There have been delays in action. All this, I must try now to correct."

He began to correct them on July 11, 1878, with the removal of Chester Arthur in the New York Customhouse. He had been threatening to do so since the first few months of his administration, but in typical calm Hayes fashion, he waited for just the right moment.

In a little over six months, the showdown with Conkling would be a replay of an earlier spat with an equally determined foe, General Jubal Early. And the outcome would be the same.

ACTUAL DATE UNKNOWN, 1878, WASHINGTON, DC,
ARBITRATES PEACE BETWEEN ARGENTINA AND PARAGUAY

From 1864–1870, war raged between the South American countries of Brazil, Paraguay and Argentina. The conflict, much like similar conflicts with their northern hemisphere neighbors, raged around claims to various tracts of land.

Peace was eventually settled among the three nations in 1870, with Paraguay bearing the brunt of losses at some estimates equal to 1.2 million people. Although the war had ended, peace would be negotiated separately between Brazil and Paraguay, and Argentina and Paraguay due to continued disagreements over valuable land.

Not until 1876 did Paraguay and Argentina finally come to an agreement, but still argued over a tract of land, equaling 28,150 square miles, between the countries and two of its major rivers. In 1878, the two sides asked President Hayes to arbitrate.[1] Representatives from both nations came to Washington, DC, and the president, as he had done so many times before between two 'warring' factions, considered the sides.

Due to the fact the nation of Paraguay was almost completely destroyed during the war, and were still digging out of the destruction, Hayes sympathized with the representatives, and awarded the land to Paraguay. In honor of President Hayes, Paraguay renamed the land "Presidente Hayes" and it's capital, "Villa Hayes."

The Nobel Prize for Peace would not begin to be awarded until 1901, but Rutherford Hayes would have deserved it.

1. "The Paraguayan War," last modified April 8, 2016, https://en.wikipedia.org/wiki/Paraguayan_War.

December 2, 1878, Washington, DC, Annual Message

The midterm elections did not go well for the Republicans. Promises made by southern states to allow African Americans to vote were broken. Hayes used his Annual Message to highlight the problems:

"Touching my birthday. (1878) I was never on the whole happier than I am now. My health, and that of my wife also, is very good. Our elevation has not, I am sure, turned our heads. The abuse of us and the honest but severe criticism do not sour us. I try to judge fairly as to what is said and 'to improve' all just criticism. My Administration is no doubt stronger than ever before. The appeal to the people on grounds of a non-partisan character has been successful. I must in the future be more and more careful to do only what is wise and right."

BRADY, WASHINGTON, D. C.

Hayes, March 21, 1878.

"I respectfully urge upon your attention that the congressional elections, in every district, in a very important sense, are justly a matter of political interest and concern throughout the whole country. Each State, every political party, is entitled to the share of power which is conferred by the legal and constitutional suffrage.

It is the right of every citizen, possessing the qualifications prescribed by law, to cast one unintimidated ballot, and to have his ballot honestly counted.

So long as the exercise of this power and…this right are common and equal, practically as well as formally, submission to the results of the suffrage will be accorded loyally and cheerfully, and all the departments of Government will feel the true vigor of the popular will thus expressed.

No temporary or administrative interests of Government, however urgent or weighty, will ever displace the zeal of our people in defense of the primary rights of citizenship. They understand that the protection of liberty requires the maintenance, in full vigor, of the manly methods of free speech, free press, and free suffrage, and will sustain the full authority of Government to enforce the laws which are framed to preserve these inestimable rights.

The material progress and welfare of the States depend on the protection afforded to their citizens. There can be no peace without such protection, no prosperity without peace, and the whole country is deeply interested in the growth and prosperity of all its parts.

While the country has not yet reached complete unity of feeling and reciprocal confidence between the communities so lately and so seriously estranged, I feel an absolute assurance that the tendencies are in that direction, and with increasing force. The power of public opinion will override all political prejudices, and all sectional or State attachments, in demanding that all over our wide territory the name and character of citizen of the United States shall mean one and the same thing, and carry with them unchallenged security and respect."

January 25, 1879, Washington, DC, Pension Arrears Act

One of the promises made by President Hayes was to look after the disabled veteran. He fulfilled that promise on January 25, 1879, signing the Pension Arrears Act which allowed disabled veterans to apply for back pay to the date of honorable discharge.[1]

Although the bill was passed by conniving congressman believing it would spell doom on the government coffers and the president would have egg on his face, Hayes could care less. The men he served beside and witnessed the wounds inflicted needed help, and he was happy to follow through.[2]

1. Hoogenboom, *Rutherford B. Hayes, Warrior and President*, 378.
2. Ibid.

February 3, 1879, Washington, DC, Hayes Defeats Conkling

Almost two years into his term, Hayes had cornered Conkling. The story from his diary, though spread out over many months compared to his pursuits with General Crook, read like a battle review when spliced together as such:

"December 9, 1877—I am now in a contest on the question of the right of Senators to dictate or control nominations. Mr. Conkling insists that no officer shall be appointed in New York without his consent, obtained previously to the nomination. This is the first and most important step in the effort to reform the civil service. It now becomes a question whether I should not insist that all who receive important places should be on the right side of this vital question.

December 12, 1877—In the language of the press, 'Senator Conkling has won a great victory over the Administration.' My New York nominations were rejected, thirty-one to twenty-five. But the end is not yet. I am right, and shall not give up the contest.

March 18, 1878—Mr. Conkling in the Senate remarked that the President had one-sixth of the legislative power of the United States Government. I suppose he means that the Senate, House, and President having the whole power, and the President and one-third of either house being half, the result is— [stops?]

December 8, 1878—Now for the civil service in case the New York appointments are confirmed. The first step in any adequate and permanent reform is the divorce of the legislature from the nominating power. With this, reform can and will successfully proceed. Without it, reform is impossible.

When the New York nominations are confirmed, in case that is the result, I can go ahead with public efforts to reform the service. A special message must be prepared to go in with Mr. D. B. Eaton's report. I will make the principal point—the first point—as above indicated. Argue it fully.

The people must be educated to expect and require their Members of Congress to abstain from appointments. They must not expect them to obtain places. Congressmen must not claim to have a share of the appointments, either principal or minor places.

December 16, 1878—The political event of last week is the opposition of Conkling to the New York appointments. This is a test case. The

Senators generally prefer to confirm Merritt and Graham. But many, perhaps a majority, will not oppose Conkling on the question. Senatorial courtesy, the Senatorial prerogative, and the fear of Conkling's vengeance in future, control them. He is like Butler—more powerful because he is vindictive and not restrained by conscience.

The most noticeable weakness of Congressmen is their timidity. They fear the use to be made of their "record." They are afraid of making enemies. They do not vote according to their convictions from fear of consequences.

February 2, 1879—The contest in the Senate over the confirmation of my New York nominations for the customs offices is close and as yet undecided. If confirmed against the votes and efforts of both of the New York Senators, the decision will be of great value. It will go far to settle, 1. The right of Senators to dictate appointments. 2. It will decide in favor of keeping the offices out of politics.

February 4, 1879—We are successful. The New York nominations, Merritt and Burt, were confirmed against Arthur and Cornell after five or six hours' debate by a vote of thirty-three to twenty-four. Thirteen Republicans voted to confirm. There were two or three others who were of the same mind, but were controlled by promises. One or two would have voted with us if their votes had been needed. I will now write to General Merritt my views and wishes as to the conduct of his office."

Hayes took the victory a step further, outlining to General Merritt exactly how he wanted the ship to be sailed.

"Executive Mansion, Washington, D. C., February 4, 1879,

Dear General: —I congratulate you on your confirmation. It is a great gratification to your friends, very honorable to you, and will prove,

I believe, of signal service to the country. My desire is that your office shall be conducted on strictly business principles, and according to the rules which were adopted on the recommendation of the Civil Service Commission by the Administration of General Grant.

In making appointments and removals of subordinates, you should be perfectly independent of mere influence. Neither my recommendation, nor that of the Secretary of the Treasury, nor the recommendation of any Member of Congress, or other influential person, should be specially regarded. Let appointments and removals be made on business principles and by fixed rules."

Back to his diary:

"February 14, 1879—Let government appointments be wholly separated from congressional influence and control except as provided in the Constitution and all needed reforms of the service will speedily and surely follow. Impressed with the vital importance of good administration in all departments of government, I must do the best I can unaided by public opinion, and opposed in and out of Congress by a large part of the most powerful men in my party.

I have written a letter to General Merritt which taken with my message embodies the leading principles on which I desire the officers appointed by me to administer their offices. I will have them printed together and send them to important offices, as occasion seems to demand.

January 16, 1881—If there are any two men in the country whose opposition and hatred are a certificate of good character and sound statesmanship, they are Conkling and Butler. I enjoy the satisfaction of being fully endorsed by the hatred and opposition of both these men."

Hayes had won, and moved the power back to the President.

MARCH 1, 1879, WASHINGTON, DC, VETO THE CHINESE EXCLUSION BILL

As the 1870s closed, workers in California were becoming agitated over the influx of legal Chinese immigrants taking their jobs in the shipyards. Rutherford Hayes saw the reason behind the outrage and, as revealed below in his diary, agreed with it. But he stood up for the immigrants because they were not violating the law. The real treasure amidst the entry is the president's admission of the reputation of the United States and its treatment of minorities.

"February 20, 1879—Both houses have passed a bill intended to prevent Chinese from coming to this country in large numbers. I am satisfied the present Chinese labor invasion (it is not in any proper sense immigration—women and children do not come) is pernicious and should be discouraged.

Our experience in dealing with the weaker races—the negroes and Indians, for example,—is not encouraging. We shall oppress the Chinamen, and their presence will make hoodlums or vagabonds of their oppressors. I therefore would consider with favor suitable measures to discourage the Chinese from coming to our shores. But I suspect that this bill is inconsistent with our treaty obligations. I must carefully examine it. If it violates the National faith, I must decline to approve it.

February 23, 1879—The Chinese Bill now likely to pass both house—has passed both but is waiting action of the House on Senate amendments—attracts much attention. As I see it, our treaty with China forbids me to give it my approval. The treaty was of our seeking. It was proposed by our minister to China, Mr. Burlingame. He became the

Ambassador of China to this country, and in Washington negotiated it with Mr. Seward. It was first ratified by our Senate and sent to China for ratification there. It was applauded by all parts of this country. The Pacific Coast joined in this. It is now claimed that it has proved unsatisfactory and pernicious, and the bill in question seeks to prevent the mischiefs complained of by a measure which violates its most important provisions. We have accepted the advantages which the treaty gives us. Our traders, missionaries, and travelers are domiciled in China. Important interests have grown up under the treaty and rest upon faith in its observance.

- One of the parties to a treaty cannot rightfully by legislation violate it.
- The whole subject was thoroughly understood when this treaty was made. For twenty years the Chinamen had been coming. Complaints were made. Laws passed to prevent it. We chose to enter into the treaty. If we assume it to have been a mistaken policy, it was our policy. We urged it on China. Our minister conducted it.
- In the maintenance of the national faith, it is in my judgment a plain duty to withhold my approval from this bill. We should deal with China in this matter precisely as we expect and wish other nations to deal with us.
- All the protection which the treaty gives to Chinese subjects who have come to America in the faith of that treaty would be withdrawn. In like manner our citizens, who as missionaries and in commercial pursuits are domiciled in China, would be left without treaty protection.
- Under these articles the Chinese have the rights of the most favored nation in this country.
- We stand for the sacred observance of treaties.
- We abrogate without notice, without negotiation, the vital articles of a treaty of our own seeking, and, it may be truthfully said, of our own making. No precedent for such action except in cases which justify war.

- Grant that the results are unsatisfactory and pernicious. We make no complaint to China before taking action.

No change in facts has occurred since the treaty was made ten years ago. No new and sudden emergency has arisen. The same causes of complaint, the same facts, were then before our eyes. Our countrymen on the Pacific Coast with great unanimity and with the utmost earnestness desire a change in our relations with China. They are entitled to have, and they should have, our sympathy in this matter.

If we could put ourselves in their places it is absolutely certain that we should think and feel as they do. We should at once devise appropriate measures to give them assurance of relief. This can be done long before there is any material increase of their present difficulties without any violation of the national faith, and without any real or substantial departure from our traditional policy on the subject of immigration."

Hayes vetoed the bill, but also understood the problems which blurred on the horizon:

"February 28, 1879—The veto of the anti-Chinese bill is generally approved east of the Rocky Mountains, and bitterly denounced west of the mountains. I was burned in effigy in one town! No doubt a population without women—without wives and mothers—that can't assimilate with us, that underbids our laborers, must be hateful. It should be made certain by proper methods that such an invasion cannot permanently override our people. It cannot safely be admitted into the bosom of our American society."

The assimilation would be left for another time, and another president.

"I am convinced that it is my duty to exhaust every executive authority committed to me by the Constitution and the laws to secure to every citizen having the requisite qualifications the right to cast one unintimidated ballot and to have it honestly counted."

—*Hayes, diary, March 27, 1879*

Perhaps due to the bravado accompanying the likes of future President Theodore Roosevelt, most Americans point to the "Man With the Big Stick" as the originator of the Panama Canal. He was not. It actually began with Lincoln, and was forwarded by President Hayes. President McKinley would also have a hand in the development of the canal before Roosevelt actually started digging.

In his final year as president, Hayes was beginning to fret about national defense on two shores. And he was not afraid to pull out the Monroe Doctrine to demand American control.

"January 13, 1880—Two things that may be important have been considered. Last Friday, the 9th, I directed the Secretary of the Navy to order two of our national vessels to sail to the ports in the Chiriqui Grant, one on the Gulf of Mexico and one on the Pacific coast between Panama and the proposed Nicaragua Canal.

The purpose is to establish naval stations in these important harbors. It is claimed that an American citizen, Mr. Ambrose Thompson, has procured a very important grant of the lands surrounding these harbors, and of the right of way connecting them. Mr. Thompson conveyed to the United States, by an arrangement with President Lincoln, an interest in his grant. If it shall be deemed best by Congress to take possession of this interest, the presence of our ships and the establishing of our coaling stations will give us a foothold which will be of vast service in controlling the passage from ocean to ocean either at Panama or at Nicaragua Lake.

February 7, 1880—The most important subject now under consideration is as to the canal across the Isthmus connecting the waters of the Atlantic and the Pacific. The French engineer, Lesseps, the chief man in building the Suez Canal, is actively at work organizing, or trying to organize, a company to enter upon the work.

The time has come when the American doctrine on the subject ought to be explicitly stated. In my judgment the United States regard the commercial communication, whether by railroad or canal, between the two oceans across the Isthmus at any of the points which have been suggested, as essential to their prosperity and safety. The right of free passage at all times, in peace or war, for the purpose of commerce or for defense, the United States deem essential to their safety and prosperity.

They wish it to be understood by all concerned that the United States will not consent that any European power shall control the railroad or canal across the Isthmus of Central America. With due regard to the rights and wishes of our sister republics in the Isthmus, the United States will insist that this passageway shall always remain under American control. Whoever invests capital in the contemplated work should do it with a distinct understanding that the United States expects and intends to control the canal in conformity with its own interests.

The highway between that part of the United States which is on the Atlantic and the Gulf of Mexico, and that part of our country which is on the Pacific, must not be allowed to pass under the control of any European nation. The control must be exclusively either in the country through which it passes, or in the United States, or under the joint control of the American republics. The United States should control this great highway between that part of our country, etc., etc. This great highway must not be controlled by Europe. It must be held and controlled by America—by the American republics.

February 8, 1880—The interest of the United States in the communication—the interoceanic canal or railroad—does not rest on the Monroe Doctrine alone. That great highway connects the part of our country which is on the Atlantic with that which is on the Pacific. It is of vital importance to our prosperity and our safety. It is a part of our general system of defensive works. It is essential for national defense. It will not be permitted to pass into the control of any hostile nation. We shall deal justly with all other nations in regard to its use. We shall deal liberally with the sister American republics which are interested in the work and in the territory through which it passes. But it may as well be understood that the United States will not permit it to be held or controlled by any European nation.

February 17, 1880—The president of the Panama Railroad gave me yesterday a very interesting account of the Isthmus, of his railway, of Mr. de Lesseps and his surveys, and of the prospects of the enterprise. He thinks a canal can be built at tide level from Aspinwall to Panama; that it will not pay as an investment but would be very useful to the United States.

February 20—The true policy of the United States as to a canal across any part of the Isthmus is either a canal under American control, or no canal."

In five short weeks, President Hayes grew increasingly stubborn over this topic inside the privacy of his diary, is it possible he was as disgruntled in person? The canal would continue to be pursued by President McKinley, and realized by President Theodore Roosevelt and opened under President Wilson in 1914.

JULY 1, 1880, WASHINGTON, DC,
URGED TO RECONSIDER ONE TERM PLEDGE

President Hayes looked forward, again, to retirement and the return to Spiegel Grove. The Presidency was wearing him out.

Hayes at age fifty-nine, 1881.

June 13, 1879

"I want to get from Mr. Clark, the architect
of the Capitol, Downing's plan for laying out
as one park all of the public ground from the
Capitol to the Potomac. This has been a favorite
hobby of mine. Last night I learned from Mr.
Kasson that it is not [an] original thought
of mine—or rather that Downing long ago
urged the same thing. At the meeting of the
Monument Commission today I will talk to Mr.
Clark about it."

"*July 26, 1879*—Parton, in an article in the *Magazine of American History* says Washington was in favor of a single presidential term of seven years. [Parton writes:] 'The term of seven years is probably as long as any man can advantageously hold the Presidency. The strain upon the faculties of a good man is too severe to be longer borne and a young country must needs grow faster than an elderly mind.'

This is true. The strain is hard to bear. It grows harder as time passes.

June 6, 1880—Lucy and I have had a few minutes' talk on this laborious, anxious, slavish life. It has many attractions and enjoyments, but she agrees so heartily with me as I say: "Well, I am heartily tired of this life of bondage, responsibility, and toil. I wish it was at an end. I rejoice that it is to last only a little more than a year and a half longer."

On July 1, 1880, Republican leaders approached him about running for a second term. Now what do you suppose his answer was? The man whose direction guided him to do what was right, and always do what he said he would, why, the answer was obvious from the start.

James Abram Garfield had been nominated as a dark horse candidate in June, and Hayes was planning a trip west, the first president to visit California.

September 22, 1880, Sacramento, California,
The Three Great Principles

While on his Western Swing in Sacramento, California, President Hayes laid out his "Three Great Principles," hearkening back to the three documents he based his entire political philosophy upon since he was a child looking up to George Washington:

"Three great principles set forth in three great charters made the United States the earth's most desirable place to live.

1. The Declaration of Independence gave us 'equal rights of all men before the law'...the very foundation-stone of our institutions.

2. The Northwest Ordinance of 1787 promoted free public schools, 'If you are to have one race, equal suffrage, universal suffrage, you can only do it by having universal education.'

3. The Constitution is the perpetual union of separate states balancing one supreme nation with local self-government."[1]

Speaking to the citizens of Sacramento, Hayes said, "And now it is for you...to see that in the future, as in the past, American institutions and the American name shall lose nothing at your hands."[2]

1. Hoogenboom, *Rutherford B. Hayes, Warrior and President*, 442.
2. Ibid.

December 26, 1880

If I speak on leaving here to friends, I may perhaps at Columbus enumerate the things done or acted upon during my term—not to discuss or boast of them but merely to name them. I may speak of returning to private life as Washington and Jefferson did; not to shirk the duties of a citizen, but not expecting or seeking again to fill conspicuous offices—offices provoking competitions—but ready to do what I may in private life or in humble stations, or if generally called to higher duties.

How will you pass time? Or, that other unwarrantable phrase, 'How will you kill time?' A man with proper notions and training, with books and grounds and neighbors, and with the interests that are crowding around all who have a sense of duty to their fellow men, will have more trouble to find time for his work than to find work to occupy all the time at his command.

Sunday, January 23, 1881

"Coming in, I was denounced as a fraud by all the extreme men of the opposing party, and as an ingrate and a traitor by the same class of men in my own party. Going out, I have the good will, blessings, and approval of the best people of all parties and sections. The thing that seems to me unaccountable is that, with more than usual distrust of my own powers, I had a strong and comforting faith that I should be able to organize and conduct an Administration which would satisfy and win the country.

This faith never deserted me. I had it before either the election or the nomination. Doubtless it was founded on my experience. I have often said that I never fail to gain the confidence and friendship of those I wish to win, if I have time and an opportunity to do so."

—*Hayes, diary*

Back to Ohio...

"To perpetuate the Union and to abolish slavery were the work of war. To educate the uneducated is the appropriate work of peace."

— *Rutherford B. Hayes*

The work of Hayes was not finished. That is, the work begun in the trenches of the Civil War. He sought two outcomes—first, the education of the freemen and second, the establishment of skilled trade centers for students. Everyone, he believed, should learn a trade. "We must not divorce the mind from the hand."[1]

The essence of both beliefs are rooted in this letter:

"Washington, DC, August 16, 1880,

Dear Sir: [Unidentified]—At the great reunion of the Ohio soldiers last week I tried to show that to complete the victory gained by the Union arms it was necessary that the means of education should be amply provided for all parts of our country. Wherever universal education prevails in the United States, the results of the war are cheerfully accepted and the constitutional amendments embodying those results are inviolable. Ignorance is the enemy most to be dreaded by the friends of free government. Ignorant voters are powder and ball for the demagogues.

The right to vote will lose its value in our country if ignorance is permitted permanently to prevail in any considerable portion of it. The schoolmaster alone can abolish the evils which slavery has left in the

South. Universal education is the only safe foundation for universal suffrage. Men cannot be fitted for the duties of citizenship in a republic without free schools.

Jefferson said: 'Without education universal suffrage will be a farce or a tragedy, and perhaps both.' In too many instances elections are already the farce he predicted.

Let us hasten to provide for all our countrymen the means of instruction, that we may escape the tragedy which Jefferson predicted.

Sincerely,

R. B. Hayes"

At the first meeting of the Slater Fund, a group overseeing a million-dollar endowment from John Slater for the education of Freedmen, Hayes was elected its President. He worked tirelessly for equal rights for African Americans through equal footing with education.

1.   Hoogenboom, *Rutherford B. Hayes, Warrior and President,* 442.

SEPTEMBER 7, 1883, SARATOGA, NEW YORK,
PRESIDENT OF THE NATIONAL PRISON REFORM ASSOCIATION

Perhaps rooted in his experience in Columbus and Cincinnati as a criminal defense lawyer, Hayes was always mindful of the sordid conditions offered in the nation's prisons, and notably in Ohio.

Hayes believed in prison reform, and in his post-presidential years, navigated his time between the education of the poor, which he believed would keep them from a life of crime, and improving conditions for those that had come to the life anyway. The National Prison Reform Association would elect him their president on September 7, 1883.

He would write in October, 1885:

"October 29, Thursday—Mr. Eugene Smith of New York, lawyer, is a sincere and earnest friend of the Prison cause. His paper at Detroit on jails—'County Jails'—was excellent. His wife is a daughter of Rev. Dr. Bacon, of New Haven, and is intelligent and bright—worthy of her lineage.

The drift of Eugene Smith's paper was to show that jails were training-schools for crime—compulsory under the law, and at the public expense. He conclusively showed the grave and fatal defects of our whole jail system. The remedy is, jails in which there is complete isolation of the Prisoners,—'the Ohio Jail,' so-called, unfortunately rarely found even in Ohio. The Congress resolved against these jails."

Modern praise is heaped upon former president Jimmy Carter for his tireless work on behalf of many charities throughout the world. His one-hundred-year predecessor holds the precedent. Only Rutherford Hayes could spend so much of his remaining time helping so many people on the absolute fringes of society.

June 25, 1889, Spiegel Grove, Fremont, Ohio,
"Do you hear me, Darling?"

The Diary of Rutherford Hayes beams with love for his wife, Lucy. Far into middle age, the adoration grew. He wrote in 1880 at the Executive Mansion, "Lucy is forty-nine today. I never loved her so much as now."

On June 22, 1889, Lucy, who had struggled with illness since returning from Washington, endured a fatal stroke. Hayes records:

"June 23, Sunday—Lucy is apparently more difficult to arouse. Her face and eyes looked natural, almost with their old beauty, when Dr.

Rice tried to awaken her so she could swallow medicine. I think she failed to swallow it. But she had life in her eyes and face. Now I fear, alas! I have seen her eyes for the last time. Those glorious eyes! are they gone—forever? She still grasps my hand, I think intelligently and with the old affection. This at 7 A.M.

7:20 A.M.—Lucy opened her eyes and with a conscious grasp, as she looked in mine affectionately, responded to my inquiry, 'Do you hear me, darling?' But her eyelids do not open as they did last night!...

8 A.M. Dr. Hilbish calls. He thinks the indications rather less favorable than yesterday...She is weaker and more disposed to sleep. She now looks natural and rests quietly.

June 24. Monday, 4:40 A.M.—The end is now inevitable. I can't realize it, but I think of her as gone. Dear, darling Lucy! When I saw and heard her last in full life, she was gathering flowers for me to carry to Mary, last Monday. When she found I would be too late for my train to Toledo if I waited longer, with her cheerful voice she said: 'Oh, well, it makes no difference. I can send them (or I will send them) by express at noon.' This she did, and Mary got them. I was barely in time for the train—not a moment to lose. A characteristic act. It was like her. For me the last—oh, the last!

At 4 P. M.—Now, more than three days since the attack, finds her much in the same condition she has been since the first day. We wait.

Without pain, without the usual suffering, she has been permitted to come to the gates of the great change which leads to the life where pain and suffering are unknown.

Just as she was reaching the period when the infirmities and sufferings of mortal life are greatest, she is permitted to go beyond them all. Whatever life can give to the most fortunate, she has enjoyed to the full. How wise and just this is! If ever a man or woman found exquisite happiness in imparting happiness to others, the dear companion of my life, my Lucy, is that woman. Should I not be full of joy and gratitude for

The Hayes family at Spiegel Grove, 1888.

the good fortune which gave me her? Few men in this most important relation of life have been so blessed as I have been. From early mature manhood to the threshold of old age I have enjoyed her society in the most intimate of all relations. How all of my friends love her! My comrades of the war almost worship her.

Often I have said our last days together have been our best days. Who knows what the future might have brought to her? It is indeed hard—hard indeed—to part with her, but could I or should I call her back? Rather let me try to realize the truth of the great mystery. 'The Lord hath given, the Lord hath taken away; blessed be the name of the Lord.'

June 25, Tuesday—Lucy died without pain this morning at 6:30. All were present. I held her hand and gazed upon her fine face to the last; when, kissing her good-bye as she left the earth, I joined the dear daughter and the others children in walking on the porch in the bracing air of the lovely morning."

Lucy Hayes was fifty-seven years old, and had been married to Rutherford for thirty-six years. She bore eight children, five of whom survived past early childhood.

Emerson had his say about what mothers did for their sons, another modern quip reveals "Behind every successful man is a woman who loves him." Such was the bond of Rutherford and Lucy Hayes.

She was transformative, yet tender. She was revolutionary, but graceful. Without the crutch of alcohol her stewardship of the Executive Mansion is still talked about today. When the Architect of the Capitol kicked the children of Washington off the grounds for the annual Easter Egg Roll in 1877, Lucy Hayes welcomed them to the White House lawn, a practice still revered and enjoyed today by tens of thousands of children and families.

She was the blueprint for the affectionate term, "First Lady." Future presidents, with all due respect to the subject of this book, will find themselves walking in the giant footsteps of Washington, Lincoln, the Roosevelts, and Kennedy. But future First Ladies walk in the simple yet beautiful footsteps of Lucy Hayes.

November 23, 1892, Columbus, Ohio,
Elected President of the Board of Trustees of Ohio State

Throughout his tenure as governor and after he was president, Rutherford Hayes pushed for the establishment of The Ohio State University. As governor, he pushed the legislature to finally apply for the money available in the Morrill Act. Financing was stalled because there was confusion between the current colleges who wanted to split the funding. But Hayes insisted on a new state university. First noted as the Ohio Agricultural and Medical College in 1870, it became The Ohio State University in 1878.[1]

On November 23, 1892, the Board of Trustees honored Hayes by making him president of the university. He would serve only sixty days.

Because he was a proud Buckeye long before it became a trend, this author is certain of one thing, there would be no bigger cheerleader in modern times, heralding the academic and athletic success of the students at The Ohio State University, than Rutherford B. Hayes.

1.   Barnard, *Rutherford B. Hayes and His America*, 247.

Epilogue...

JANUARY 17, 1893, SPIEGEL GROVE, FREMONT OHIO,
"GOING WHERE LUCY IS…"

'Tis well, 'tis something, we may stand
Where he in English earth is laid
And from his ashes may be made
The violet of his native land.

'Tis little; but it looks in truth
As if the quiet bones were blest
Among familiar names to rest,
And in the places of his youth.

Come, then, pure hands, and bear the head
That sleeps or wears the mask of sleep;
And come, whatever loves to weep,
And hear the ritual of the dead.

Ah! yet, even yet, if this might be,
I, falling on his faithful heart,
Would, breathing through his lips, impart
The life that almost dies in me:

That dies not, but endures with pain,

And slowly forms the firmer mind,

Treasuring the look it cannot find,

The words that are not heard again.

—Alfred Lloyd Tennyson, In Memoriam, 1866

D arkness had fallen at Spiegel Grove when Rutherford Birchard Hayes, Jr. died in his bedroom on January 17, 1893. He was seventy years old. He had been in Cleveland four days before, promoting the Industrial Education program at Ohio State. He felt a chill, and informed his son Webb he would, "rather die at Spiegel Grove than live anywhere else."

"He has steadily grown in the public esteem, and the impartial historian will not fail to recognize the conscientiousness, the manliness, and courage that so strongly characterized his whole public career."

—President Benjamin Harrison, Eulogy

Sadly, President Harrison is wrong. Rutherford Hayes has not been recognized for his conscientiousness, manliness, and courage. Hayes is stuck in the middle of a period largely discarded by history-enthusiasts, between the excitement and turmoil of the Civil War and the rise of the imperial presidency with the dynamic and captivating Theodore Roosevelt.

Hayes preferred not to be captivating. He was calm. He did not draw

Hayes and grandson Sherman, 1892.

attention to himself. He was content with letting others speak despite his own penchant for wisdom and brevity. And although he was witty, friendly, and cheerful, his photographs, like Lincoln's, reveal only a stoic, serious face.

But why have we forgotten him? For one, there was this from a scholar in 1954:

"The succession of presidents from Grant through McKinley (with the possible exception of Cleveland) never exercised any real qualities of leadership and scarcely made a mark on history."

—*Foster Rhea Dulles,* The United States Since 1865, *1954.*

For lack of a better term, this is complete hogwash.

For this author, it was exceedingly difficult to choose just 100 days to reveal the true character and quality of the man. He served a full presidency, against a combative congress, confidently managing the government with sound financial steering, wise checking of the congress by never abusing his constitutional authority, all the while navigating the wicked waters of politics by treating everyone, including his adversaries with quiet, sometimes undeserved respect.

Forgive this author for vehemently denouncing any inference that Hayes had no qualities of leadership. It begs the question just what history Dulles was reading at the time, though it was in this same period Arthur Schlesinger Jr. was tinkering with his presidential ranking system where the value of Hayes was scandalously low.

Hayes himself saw the period of his presidency with the eyes of a prophet in 1871 when he admitted he had no interest in the United States Senate because the work of his life was largely done. In his diary on March 16, 1871, he said, "the small questions of today about taxation, appointments, etc., etc., are petty and uninteresting." In other words, he found it all very boring. Perhaps the scholars, professors, and students of history since 1893 do, too.

But six years after he dismissed politics altogether, he was president of the United States. The country desperately needed his steady right hand on the issues of equality, sound money, discrimination, and political greed.

The purpose of this book is to spark new interest in Hayes and to promote further research into his incredible life. The purpose is not to confront the one hundred twenty-three years of historical scholarship which has cast him aside. But the mountain of redemption is tempting. First, consider the reasons why Hayes is not among the likes of Washington, Lincoln, and Franklin Roosevelt:

He served one term. Hayes promised to serve only one term in his address accepting the nomination of the Republican party as a way to prove appointments in his administration would be on the basis of qualifications and not political expediency. He took a bold step forward in his inaugural address by advocating future presidents be limited to one six-year term for the same reason.

Unfortunately, Hayes was far ahead of his time. And although the twenty-second amendment would limit the president to two terms in 1951, primarily to prevent another Roosevelt dynasty, the days of completely divorcing the president from political favors are still far ahead of us.

Leadership with the Veto. One hundred years before President George H. W. Bush was begging for a line-item veto to cut pork barrel spending, President Hayes repeatedly vetoed legislation written by an antagonistic congress. He vetoed thirteen bills, some as easy as the Chinese Exclusion Act and many due to their exclusion of funds to support the rights of African Americans to vote in the south. Vetoes, in the course of American history, do not ring like *The Civil Rights Act of 1965*, or the *Americans with Disabilities Act of 1990*. Vetoes are stubborn, pitting one man—the president—against the majority rule of Congress.

But Hayes used his veto power cautiously, albeit frequently. Congress was determined to squash the civil and economic rights of African and Chinese Americans in the late 1870s, and President Hayes was defiant against it. If standing up for the rights of minority citizens is not leadership at its finest, then the preamble to the Constitution means nothing.

The Election Question. The election of 1876 cast a deep, dark shadow over President Hayes which is wholly undeserved and unnecessary. But such is politics. Hayes is often cast as moving behind the scenes to assure the votes in Florida and Oregon fall in his category. After reading his diary and letters of the same period, this is most certainly not the case.

Furthermore, the Potter Commission—designed to uncover Republican cases of fraud in the election and cast doubt on the legitimacy of President Hayes—completely backfired on the Democrats, who discovered rampant fraud on their own side in the election.

Rutherford Hayes counseled his associates thusly: "There must be nothing crooked on our part." Tragically, the honest, upright legacy of Hayes is tormented by slogans and nicknames which are easier to remember than facts.

Hayes himself outlined his own list of accomplishments as he looked at one year remaining on his term, April 11, 1880:

"If I were to here enumerate the points in which the Administration has been successful in a marked degree I would name:
1. Judicial appointments. Mr. Justice Harlan, Supreme Court
2. Foreign Missions. Andrew D. White
3. Cabinet-able gentlemen, free from scandals.
4. No nepotism in the President's appointments.
5. Good morals in the White House.
6. Maintaining the authority of the President in appointments against congressional dictation, and especially against Senatorial dictation.

7. Maintaining sound doctrine in vetoes of bills designed to coerce the Executive.

8. Veto of Chinese Bill.

9. Veto of Silver Bill.

10. Firm adherence to resumption and successfully carrying it out.

11. The Mexican policy, securing peace and safety on the Texas border.

12. The true doctrine asserted as to European control of an Isthmus canal.

13. An Indian policy [of] justice and fidelity to engagements, and placing the Indians on the footing of citizens.

14. A constitutional, just, and liberal policy upon the Southern question.

15. Non-partisan appointments in greater number than any President since Washington. Key in the Cabinet, a marshal for Georgia, a judge for District of Columbia, a commissioner of District of Columbia, members of Board of Health, of Mississippi River Commission, visitors to West Point and Annapolis, Minister to Brazil; postmasters, many, census supervisors. Several hundred in all.

16. The prompt and firm suppression of the great riots of 1877.

17. Raids into the Indian Territory prevented.

18. The true policy with respect to Mormonism and polygamy.

19. The Administration has never had a newspaper organ in Washington or elsewhere. As Mr. Evarts said: 'The Administration has not been well edited.' This is good as a joke, but with the newspapers so enterprising and able as they now are, no organ is wisdom. It gives all a fair chance, and gives the Administration a fair chance with all.

20. In fine, I have not done as much to improve the system and methods of the civil service as I hoped and tried to do, but I have improved the service in all of its branches until it is equal to any in the world—equal to that of any previous Administration. Look at its purity, efficiency, freedom from scandals, and decide as to its merits."

From here, permit this author to predict a bold measure: With an accurate re-appraisal of Rutherford Hayes in the coming years, Schlesinger's rankings will place Hayes solidly in the top ten, side-by-side with our greatest presidents. If this book sparks our re-acquaintance with this extraordinary man, our history will be that much more complete.

President Hayes should also be remembered for his encouragement and promotion of three anchors in the vista of Washington, DC. He resurrected the idea of a National Mall, he restarted the completion of the Washington monument, which was stalled due to a lack of financial resources, and focused much-needed attention on the nation's library and the buildings housing it.

Add to the aesthetic anchors, the White House Easter Egg Roll and the cultural legacy of White House entertainment long before First Lady Jaqueline Kennedy, the Hayes administration should stand proudly beside the pillars of our nation's history for a wide variety of important reasons.

Finally, consider the topics of the vulgar 2016 presidential campaign:

- Equal rights for our citizens.
- Minority discrimination and harassment.
- Anti-immigration sentiment.
- Big business influence on government.
- Party influence on government policies.
- Angry workers demanding higher wages.

Is this 2016 or 1876?

We could certainly use a lot more Hayeses in our country today, couldn't we? Consider the issues Hayes raised his entire political life, and the issues he spent his final years in complete devotion:

- Equal opportunity for education regardless of race or class.
- Industrial training for our high school and college students.
- Reform of our prisons.
- Reform of asylums and hospitals.
- Equal rights.

President Nixon was fond of saying, "The finest steel goes through the hottest fire." Rutherford Hayes lived his entire life in that fire. He could have died under the ice that day at Kenyon College or been killed countless times on the battlefield in the Kanawha Valley. And for that matter he could have given up any number of times throughout his very difficult life. But time and time again, he refused to give up. And he refused to allow others less fortunate to give up, too.

Perhaps today, with the world in such chaos and uncertainty around us, we can look at the extraordinary life of Rutherford Hayes and sincerely believe—as he made it through the fire—we can, too.

"Two-thousand sixteen marks the 100th anniversary of the nation's first presidential library, The Rutherford B. Hayes Library and Museum in Fremont, Ohio, on the grounds of his beloved Spiegel Grove. The Hayes home is lovingly and beautifully restored to the time period of the 1880s, when Rutherford and Lucy returned from Washington, DC.

The library and research center, fresh off a 1.5-million-dollar renovation, is one of the finest museums in the nation to glimpse a former president up close and personal. Please visit Spiegel Grove. Reflect, learn, and come away rejuvenated by the story of a man who deserves a place in history, if not higher on the scholarly scale, a lot higher in our own esteem. Spiegel Grove will show you why."

—*Eric Ebinger, 2016*

The Twenty-Five Rules of Hayes

Sadly, Rutherford Hayes is widely known for only one sentence from his inaugural address. As this book was researched, I found myself jotting down quotes I felt could stand alone as rules by which to live—a personal exercise running parallel to the research. As the list grew, I decided to include it here. We memorize Lincoln and Roosevelt and Kennedy. It is time we give the words Hayes lived by their equal measure.

1. Keep cool—to treat all adversaries considerately, respectfully, and kindly, but...to satisfy them of my sincerity and firmness.
2. I do not defend mistakes in methods. I do not insist on my own particular plans. If better plans are proposed, I shall be ready to support them. But the important ends must not be abandoned.
3. You can't but fight one battle at a time, two at the most.
4. Absolute and complete divorce from your inkstand. No letters to strangers or anybody else on politics.
5. We must not divorce the mind from the hand. Let the normal instruction be that men must earn their own living, and that by the labor of their hands as far as may be. This is the gospel of salvation for the colored man. Let the labor not be servile, but in manly occupations like those of the carpenter, the farmer, and the blacksmith.
6. A good cause often suffers by the reckless and baseless statements of its injudicious and excitable friends.
7. Be a good scholar if you can, but in any event be a gentleman in the best sense of the word—truthful, honorable, polite and kind with the golden rule as your guide. Do nothing that would give pain to your mother if she knew it.

8. Men in political life must be ambitious. But the surest path to the White House is his who never allows his ambition to get there to stand in the way of any duty, large or small.

9. Do not let your bachelor ways crystallize so that you can't soften them away when you come to have a wife and family of your own.

10. Whoever interferes with equal rights and equal opportunities is in some sense in some real degree responsible for the crimes committed in the community.

11. Must swear off...swearing.

12. What do we want? We want confidence. Do not encourage your Legislature or your Congress to legislate too much. It was a favorite maxim with Jefferson that the world was governed too much. Too much legislation on financial subjects is the bane of our times. My friends, let us all hold up our hands in favor of letting well enough alone, and standing firmly by our present Constitutional currency. That destroys no man. *The Toledo Address, September 19, 1878.*

13. My Dear Boy: [Birchard]—You ask me about the college at Hudson [Western Reserve]. It has a good history—has turned out many able and successful men. I hope it will grow into a great institution. I have no doubt you can get there all that is essential which any college can give. You will hear no objection from me if it is finally thought best by you and Uncle to go to that college. But I prefer you would not finally decide about it until I have a talk with both of you. You can, if you wish, go on and study as if that would be your college. In a few weeks I will see you and Uncle and consider all sides. The main thing is the student—his industry, his habits, character, and talents. The college affords him merely the tools. *Columbus, Ohio, March 11, 1870.*

14. He who lives a great truth is incomparably greater than he who but speaks it. *April 10, 1871.*

15. Now, my son, I need not urge you to give solid and honest work to your studies. Whatever the line of business you pursue in life, training

that hard study will give you will be of service to you. Try to understand fully whatever you go over. Thoroughness is the vital thing. More important than study, however, is honesty, truthfulness, and sincerity. Resolve to abide by these under all circumstances, and keep the resolution. Such a character as you will then have will make you honored and happy, and your parents proud of and fond of you. A little too much sermon! From your affectionate father, R. B. Hayes.

16. I have a talent for silence and brevity. I can keep silent when it seems best to do so, and when I speak I can, and do usually, quit when I am done. This talent, or these two talents, I have cultivated. Silence and concise, brief speaking have got me some laurels, and, I suspect, lost me some. No odds. Do what is natural to you, and you are sure to get all the recognition you are entitled to. *November 20, 1872.*

17. Keep on the sunny side in cold weather. Even the coldest of us has a sunny side if one could only discover it. *February 12, 1875 to son Webb.*

18. I once in a while feel as if I might be called away suddenly. If so, I want all of my boys to remember as my last words to them: Always be honest in both deed and word; and always be thoughtful, considerate, kind in your treatment of your mother. I do not think any of you are lacking in integrity or goodness to your mother, but I mention these two points to impress them on your minds. Don't forget them as you respect me, and as you wish to deserve happiness—and to deserve it is the surest way to have it. *June 13, 1870.*

19. Don't work too hard until this torrid weather leaves us. I inherit a Presbyterian fatalism. We shall get through, if we are to do it. *To Carl Schurz: Columbus, Ohio, July 24, 1876.*

20. It is to be hoped that as my past and my letters and speeches, a few of which are published in Howard's "Life," are examined, the people will find that I am likely to be one of the last men in the world to back out of a good work, deliberately entered upon. *To Carl Schurz: Columbus, Ohio, August 9, 1876.*

21. After talk of 100,000 dollars needed to carry Indiana in the presidential election, Hayes said in his diary, "I mean to go through cheerfully and firmly and with clean hands. If defeated, there will be no bitterness in the disappointment, and I shall have my self-respect and an approving conscience."

22. The one thought I would like to lodge in all minds is, Keep out of debt. If in debt, now is the time to get out of it in the only safe way, by honestly paying them. The honest payment of debts is the safest way to get rid of them. But let every man, every corporation, and especially let every village, town, and city, every county and State, get out of debt and keep out of debt. It is the debtor that is ruined by hard times.

23. I am glad my boys voted. To vote is like the payment of a debt—a duty never to be neglected, if its performance is possible. *October 14, 1879.*

24. If I talk to the soldiers, why not speak of the fruits of their services on the right side of the good cause? It is now true that this is God's country, if equal rights, a fair start, and an equal chance in the race of life are everywhere secured to all. If clouds cast their shadows on our path, we are cheered also by the sunlight of prosperity. What is our condition now? The debt, failures, incomes, employment for skilled and common labor at fair prices—a fair day's wage for a fair day's work. What we fought for was to make us one people—a free people with an equal start and a fair chance in the race.

    Just in proportion as the results and true principles of that combat have been fully and cheerfully accepted, just in that proportion is our country in its several parts prosperous and happy. *July 25, 1880.*

25. If a thing ought to be done according to the lights we have, let us go and do it, leaving events to take care of themselves. *July 24, 1862.*

Selected Bibliography

This book is based upon the diary and letters of Rutherford B. Hayes, which are located online and at the Rutherford B. Hayes Library and Museum in Fremont, Ohio.

Books

Barnard, Harry, *Rutherford B. Hayes and his America*, Newtown, Connecticut, American Political Biography Press, 1954.

Bellesiles, Michael A., 1877, *America's Year of Living Violently*, New York, New York, The New Press, 2010.

Geer, Emily Apt, *First Lady, The Life of Lucy Webb Hayes*, Akron, Ohio, Kent State University Press, 1984.

Hoogenboom, Ari, *Rutherford B. Hayes, Warrior and President*, Lawrence, Kansas, University Press of Kansas, 1995.

Hoogenboom, Ari, *One of the Good Colonels*, Abilene, Texas, McWhiney Foundation Press, 1999.

Perry, James M., *Touched With Fire*, New York, New York, Public Affairs™, 2003.

Truman, Margaret, *The President's House*, New York, New York, Random House, 2003.

Newspapers

Cincinnati Commercial Tribune
Cincinnati Intelligencer
Daily Ohio Statesman
Daily Graphic

INDEX

"Once in about twenty years a campaign on personal characteristics is in order. General Jackson in 1820–24 [1824–28], General Harrison in 1840, Lincoln in 1860, now Garfield in 1880. I know we can't repeat in details, but in substance we can. In this instance we stand on the rock of truth. Such struggles with adverse circumstances and such success! The boy on the tow-path has become in truth the scholar and the gentleman by his own unaided work. He is the ideal candidate because he is the ideal self-made man. If he were not in public life he would be equally eminent as a professor in a college, as a lecturer, as an author, an essayist, or a metaphysician."

—*Rutherford Hayes on*
James Garfield, June 11, 1880

 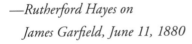

Eric Ebinger was raised in an old farmhouse in the Firelands of north central Ohio. Ignited with a "passion for presidents" by his great grandmother and nurtured by the rest of his family, Ebinger began studying American History—specifically presidents—at the age of eleven. Ebinger graduated from Penn State University in 1999 with a Bachelor of Arts in History. He is the author of the 2014 novel *The Presidents Gather*, a fictional account of how past presidents would have reacted to the attacks on the United States on September 11, 2001.

As well as writing this series of biographical *100 Days* books on the presidents, he is the host of a YouTube Channel called "The Lincoln Traveler." He still lives in the Firelands with his wife Misty, a brood of chickens, and a Boxer Dog named Lincoln. Follow him at EricEbinger.com.